SOUTH AFRICA

HOOVER INTERNATIONAL STUDIES
Richard F. Staar, general editor

THE PANAMA CANAL CONTROVERSY
Paul B. Ryan

THE IMPERIAL REVOLUTIONARIES
Hugh Seton-Watson

SOUTH AFRICA: WAR, REVOLUTION, OR PEACE?
L. H. Gann and Peter Duignan

SOUTH AFRICA

*War
Revolution
or Peace?*

L. H. Gann
Peter Duignan

Hoover Institution Press
Stanford University, Stanford, California

Hoover Institution Publication 199

© 1978 by the Board of Trustees of the
   Leland Stanford Junior University
All rights reserved
International Standard Book Number: 0-8179-6992-6
Library of Congress Catalog Card Number: 78–59131
Printed in the United States of America

TYPESET BY TED LIGDA, REDWOOD CITY, CALIFORNIA

Contents

Tables and Figures

Foreword

The Republic of South Africa today is one of the world's most criticized states. Less than thirty years ago, however, its citizens prided themselves on having stood by Great Britain during the crucial years of World War II between 1939 and 1941 when both the United States and the USSR remained neutral in the struggle against Nazi Germany. South Africa's gold helped to sustain the British war effort, and command of the Cape represented the *sine qua non* for defense of the Middle East. But once the Third Reich had been defeated, the international climate of public opinion began to change. Today the Republic of South Africa is widely regarded by the world community as a neo-fascist power, oppressed by a bigoted pigmentocracy. Sooner or later, its critics say, white tyranny will crumble. Unless the whites surrender power soon, allegedly there will be turmoil and racial strife until war or revolution leads to a new peace.

L. H. Gann and Peter Duignan, both distinguished historians with extensive publishing records and wide experience in Africa, take a new look at this controversial subject. Their conclusions present a striking challenge to the orthodoxy of the editorial column, the lecture room, and the church pulpit. While they are critical of South Africa, they do not regard the Republic as one of the world's most oppressive regimes. As they point out, something like a million and a half black Africans have voted with their feet by coming from abroad to gain employment in that country.

It is a pleasure to introduce this monograph as the third volume in the Hoover Institution's new International Studies series. Previous books have dealt with the Panama Canal controversy and trends in world communism during the 1960s and 1970s. This publication is especially timely, since the subject of Africa is of so much interest to both government and the informed public. It should contribute to the current debate of U.S. policies toward South Africa.

RICHARD F. STAAR
Coordinator of International Studies
Hoover Institution

Stanford, California

Preface

Few countries have acquired greater unpopularity during the last three decades than South Africa. The critics of South Africa differ widely among themselves, but most of them have one thing in common. They charge that the South African system depends on a reactionary pigmentocracy that has turned color privileges for a minority into an article of faith. The country is thought to be governed by a neofascist regime that shackles freedom of thought and enslaves the nonwhite majority. The mass of the people are supposedly getting poorer, if not in absolute terms, then at least in comparison with the privileged whites. South Africa, therefore, is a danger to international peace and an affront to the dignity of man. The United States has a special responsibility: American power, diplomatic, economic, moral, even military, should be used to break the fetters of brown and black people in South Africa. The Carter administration sees the civil-rights struggle in the United States as relevant to South African racial problems. South Africa, in its view, is merely the unreconstructed South writ large, and like the Old South, South Africa must be coerced into joining the world of racial equality and integration.

The Carter administration accordingly has increased diplomatic pressure on South Africa. The United States has joined with other Western countries to attempt an arms embargo against South Africa coupled with political pressure to get the South Africans to reform their policy. The United States has called for changes in the South African political structure. An unidentified specialist in the administration has acknowledged that to muster sufficient international support the United States should take tougher measures than just backing an arms embargo. An "embargo South Africa" policy appeals to American policy makers on two opposing grounds. A South

African revolution is inevitable, it is argued; hence the United States should speed up this desirable event by aligning itself with the likely winners. Alternately, the interventionists claim, a South African revolution would result in a racial Armageddon; this would be so apocalyptic an event that United States policy should aim at aborting it by promoting peaceful political and social change in Africa.

The call for moral intervention finds support among a variety of American interest groups—radicals, establishment churches, university faculty and students and news media—and among wide segments of the federal bureaucracy.[1] A "forward" policy also appeals to militant black congressmen, black American nationalists, and what might be called the "neoabolitionist" lobby in this country, composed of liberal-minded men and women who regard South Africa as the world's last remnant of reactionary racism. The "neoabolitionists," in other words, consider the battle against the existing South African establishment as yet another chapter of the civil-rights struggle in America, and even moderate journals have begun to speak their language. The *New York Times* has argued in an editorial that President Carter's policy toward South Africa will increase American prestige in the rest of Africa, and will unite the American people behind this country's exertions overseas (see the *New York Times*, 17 May 1977).

We disagree with many of these assumptions and assertions. South Africa is not part of the United States; it is not Africa's "Deep South," but economically by far the most developed part of the African continent. Black South Africans—Zulu, Sotho, Tswana, and others—are not like black Americans. Blacks in the United States are English-speaking Americans, like most of their white neighbors; Zulu and Tswana, by contrast, form separate ethnic communities that are culturally quite distinct from those of South African whites or Indians. In many respects, South Africa resembles a multiethnic community such as Cyprus or even the old Austro-Hungarian Empire far more than the United States. It is like other African countries split by ethnic rivalries and populated by backward, tribal peoples. South Africa's problems cannot, therefore, be resolved along American lines.

The present study seeks to provide an alternative interpretation. We hope that it will suggest to policy makers options more realistic than those generally advocated by the academic establishment. We are aware that our views are far from fashionable, but we are convinced that they deserve to be heard.

We should like to express our thanks to Professors Henry Bienen, Kenneth W. Grundy, Thomas Karis, Edwin S. Munger, and Captain Paul Ryan, U.S. Navy retired. Their willingness to read our manuscript does not, of course, imply approval of our views.

1

South Africa: A Pariah State?

Its government is feared by its neighbors because it has promoted violence in the countries around it and has oppressed its people. Thousands have fled this nation, and thousands more suffer in prison. It has been called by some a threat to world peace. There are no civil liberties within its borders, and a vast network of secret police and informers cows the populace. It is ruled by a small, tightly knit, ideologically fanatic group. Those who have escaped or been freed from its prisons tell of torture, brainwashing, and poor living conditions. Yet the country's leaders profess their "correctness," defy world opinion, and continually attack the United States. A description of South Africa? No, it is Cuba. Yet most readers would have assumed that South Africa was being described. Why?

South Africa is condemned for what is often overlooked elsewhere. A double standard is being used by critics who censure South Africa for oppressing its people but do not attack other African states that do even worse. Their justification, according to a *New York Times* editorial of 14 November 1977, is that South Africa is unique in its racial suppression and therefore clearly deserving of blame. While we agree that South Africa should be censured, we hold that so should all unjust societies that oppress their people for whatever reasons. The Russians clearly discriminate against the peoples of Central Asia and even segregate them, but they mask the fact by putting up a front of racial equality. South Africa has the defect of maintaining racial inequality overtly and blatantly. Hence outsiders are not interested in examining the general condition of people within the republic. White South Africans also suffer from the fact that as persons of a Western, Christian culture, they are expected to attain a higher ethical standard than others.

In the past year, rioting in African townships such as Soweto, the deaths of twenty people in prison—particularly the beating to death of Steve Biko—the arrest and banning of black leaders, and the suppression of black organizations, have outraged world opinion and led to an arms embargo against South Africa sponsored by the United Nations. Recent attacks have been intense, but South Africa has been becoming increasingly unpopular during the last thirty years. Yet a generation ago South Africans prided themselves on having stood by Great Britain during the crucial years of World War II—1939 to 1941—when both the United States and the USSR were neutral in the struggle against Nazi Germany. South Africa's gold helped to sustain the British war effort. South Africa's command of the Cape was a sine qua non for the defense of the Middle East. But once Germany was overthrown, the international climate of opinion began to change rapidly. In 1947, for instance, Arthur Keppel-Jones, a distinguished South African historian now living in exile, published a book entitled *When Smut Goes* in which he predicted the country's coming breakdown. Liberal-minded academics, journalists, clergymen, TV commentators, and other opinion makers have been predicting South Africa's impending demise ever since. The sense of drama has been heightened of late by South Africa's nuclear potential, and even a *National Review* contributor could look with dismay to an atomic *Götterdämmerung* in the South Atlantic.

On any objective scale that ranks the "badness" of regimes, however, South Africa would not rank at the top or even near the top. It would obviously fall below the fanatic Khmer Rouge in Cambodia in terms of oppression of its people. Almost all communist states oppress and exploit their people more than does South Africa. The sentences to forced labor, imprisonments, killings, and enforced population movements of the Soviet Union or Communist China have been infinitely worse than anything whites have done to blacks in South Africa. Perhaps as many as eighty million people have died in Soviet forced-labor camps and prisons or have been murdered by communist authorities since 1917, according to Alexander Solzhenitsyn. During the Second World War entire ethnic groups—the Volga Germans and the Crimean Tartars, for instance—were brutally transplanted and decimated. After that war the Soviet Union expelled more than a million Poles from the lands it wrested from Poland, and put six million Ukrainians into forced-labor camps. Millions of refugees were forced to flee from Pakistan to India after the breakdown of the British Raj, and millions more fled from India to Pakistan. Algeria rid itself of most of its Europeans, and Uganda of its Asians. The fates of these victims were determined solely by the accident of their ethnic affinity.

These enforced population movements were so huge in scale that they make South Africa's apartheid measures seem insignificant, yet we have normal relations with most of the states that were responsible for this systematic discrimination and these mass expulsions. We seek to deal with communist regimes; we even work toward a détente with them. Churchmen no longer lead protest movements against "Godless Communism"; few leftist students or university teachers cry out for the protection of human rights in the Soviet Union, let alone in North Korea, East Germany, or Vietnam. The liberal left argues that we should "understand" the communists, that we should not "provoke" them, and that we should try to soften their regimes by promoting trade and cultural relations, by extending loans on easy terms, and by open or concealed subsidies. This is not the case with South Africa, however; for that nation world opinion—or what passes as such—instead demands sanctions, boycotts, and cultural isolation.

In addition, South Africa does not rank high among the tyrants in military and police expenditures. It spends a smaller percentage (5.1) of its gross national product (GNP) on defense than does Britain or the United States (5.4)—not to speak of East Germany (5.3), the Soviet Union (12.0), or Nigeria (7.9). Until the 1970s South Africa's entire police force was smaller than the police force of New York City, and it had to control twenty-four million people—not eight million—in an area bigger than the whole of Western Europe. Even now the South African police has less than fifty-five thousand men. The South African army, to date, has not been used to crush any African opposition movement or even to move against rioting mobs, but military force has been repeatedly used in this manner in Poland, East Germany, Hungary, Communist China, Cambodia, and Vietnam. Recent press accounts suggest that over a thousand people were executed in the last year by the Chinese army, yet no worldwide protests have condemned this brutality and no one calls for China's expulsion from the UN.

Even within the African continent, South Africa cannot be given the "highest marks" for oppression and exploitation. The claimants for the title are numerous—Uganda, Ethiopia, the Sudan, Burundi, Guinea, Angola, Mozambique, and Equatorial Guinea, to mention only the top contenders. Clearly Uganda's bloody tyrant Amin would win the contest if it were held today, with Equatorial Guinea's Nguema running a close second. But a few years ago the Sudan, Burundi, or Nigeria would have "outscored" Uganda because of the amount of genocidal bloodshed that occurred in these countries. Amin may have killed as many as three hundred thousand people, but almost that many were slain in Burundi. To date no UN or Organization of African Unity (OAU) resolution has condemned any of these states. South Africa is rightly attacked for the twenty prisoners who died under suspicious circumstances in its prisons last year; yet one man—by his own admission—killed that many in a single week in one prison in Uganda.

One can understand, if not accept, the reasons why black governments harshly attack South Africa but say nothing about Amin or other bloody tyrants in Africa. They are racially united, determined to end the last vestige of white rule on the continent; no matter what the whites did, they would not be accepted as the rightful rulers of any state in Africa. Black rage stems from a sense of powerlessness and anger at the fact that blacks are still under whites anywhere on the continent. They do not appear to mind oppression of blacks by blacks, but only condemn such conduct by whites. A racist kind of morality lets them justify black tyranny, but they never justify any kind of white governance. Thus they do not cry out against injustice as such, but only against white injustice.

Any informed person can understand why Africans should condemn South Africa and apply double standards to the white regimes, but it is not clear why we and our allies should do so. Nyerere of Tanzania has forcibly moved over three million people from their homelands in order to control them better in *Ujama* villages; South Africa has not transplanted people on this scale, but it is being bitterly attacked for its actions. Nyerere is not.

The intellectuals of the West, then, are guilty of applying double standards; they judge South African whites in terms of an absolute morality, while judging blacks according to a relative morality. Whites in South Africa must conform to Western democratic standards of civil liberties and political governance; blacks in Africa are not required to abide by these rules. One-party black governance is necessary and correct; one-party rule or one-race rule by whites is unjust. The arrest and suppression of political parties, a common practice in most black states, is justified by the real or assumed need to hold ethnic groups together. In South Africa, however, a multiethnic as well as a multiracial country, repressive means are not justified.

Make no mistake about it, South Africa has a racist, authoritarian regime. We will not defend all aspects of its governance, but neither can we justify what has occurred in most African countries and in all communist countries. Blacks, Indians, and Coloureds in South Africa have but limited political rights and civil liberties. They labor under a multitude of civic and political disabilities. They are not full citizens. They can be arrested arbitrarily and held without trial and on no charges. They suffer discrimination in jobs, housing, and education, in land ownership, and in business opportunities. They are denied equality and given only limited chances to succeed. They often live in inferior, segregated areas, with poorer public services than those of the whites. Blacks are especially subject to countless pass controls.

Most of the problems and abuses found in South Africa are also found in the rest of Africa, however; indeed they occur in much of the world. This is understandable. South Africa is an African country; it is not like Great Britain or the United States. One-party regimes are the norm in Africa; there are twenty-one of them, nineteen dictatorships, and only a few so-called multiparty states. Africa has had about fifty coups since 1960. Most African nations have preventive-detention laws that are used with the utmost ruthlessness against the opposition. (Ironically, President Nyerere, one of the strongest critics of South Africa and an honored visitor to Washington, placed more than a hundred Namibians in preventive detention merely because they disagreed with the South-West African Peoples' Organization —SWAPO—official faction.) South Africa likewise resembles the rest of Africa in that its politics are overwhelmingly ethnic; the Kikuyu or the Luo in Kenya are as much concerned with their respective ethnic positions within the state as are the different peoples of South Africa.

Africa now leads the world in the number of its refugees, and only a few thousand of these are from South Africa. Minorities—Indians, whites, other Africans—have been expelled from states such as Angola, Mozambique, Ghana, Nigeria, Uganda, Kenya, and Tanzania. Government ownership is the rule in most African states, as are large state bureaucracies. Because of ethnic diversity, all African states are fragile, so South Africa is not all that different; its major divergence lies in the domination of its black majority by the white minority. Elsewhere in Africa the black elite dominates the black majority. In the realm of civil liberties, South Africa would get about an average score. Unlike most independent African countries, it has a free, critical press—few African countries do. It has white opposition parties, an independent judiciary, and procedural justice in the courts. Property is secure; no Indian businessmen in Durban or Johannesburg would prefer black rule of the Tanzanian or Ugandan variety to South African white rule.

Critics of South Africa make much of the industrial color bar and of disparities between the wages of whites and blacks. They have a case, but they greatly exaggerate it. In 1976 less than 3 percent of all jobs were officially limited to whites, and in 1978 job restrictions were officially ended. The industrial color bar continues to erode as manufacturing concerns require an increasing number of skilled workers. Disparities in salary between blacks and whites are considerable, but the wage gap partially marks the differences in remuneration for managerial, skilled, and unskilled workers. Europeans form a large portion of the managerial and technically qualified labor force; hence their wages appear high. The problem of the wage gap is not purely South African, however; it is to be found in every African country, and it derives from a prevalent scarcity of skills. South African business, scientific, and technical personnel certainly receive a good deal less than the host of international experts working in Africa on comparable assignments under UN or other international auspices.

The bulk of white South Africans are not capitalists. (Only about 18 percent of the whites are independent entrepreneurs; the rest make their livings from wages and salaries.) White wealth is not stolen from the blacks.

The nation's economic prosperity is due to white capital, entrepreneurship, and skills as well as to black labor and enterprise. The average earnings of a black industrial worker in South Africa are three to four times greater than those of a black in Nigeria, Tanzania, or Zaïre. For example, a relatively highly paid person in Uganda (for instance, a civil-service clerk) makes $125 a month; a black truck driver in South Africa gets $250 a month plus subsidized housing. Black miners in South Africa start at $140 a month (plus free housing, medical care, and food); miners in Sierra Leone receive $50, and in Nigeria, $75 to $80. Slums and squatter settlements like the one recently destroyed outside Cape Town are not unique to South Africa. All African cities have them, and there are fewer in South Africa than anywhere else on the continent. In Addis Ababa, for example, slums account for 90 percent of all housing, and in Nairobi squatters account for 30 to 35 percent of the population.

South Africa's problems basically stem from the fact that the four million whites are surrounded by nineteen million blacks, perhaps half of whom remain poor and technologically backward and do not share the values, morals, and technical knowledge of Western man. About half the blacks have left the tribal world, and not all of these have become Westernized.

South Africans do not accept the notion that majority rule is necessarily just, or that, in their situation, "one man, one vote" will produce democracy. White South Africans are only too conscious of the fact that the normal form of government in Africa is a one-party dictatorship or military rule in which opposition groups enjoy no political rights. They are equally concerned with the danger that a national breakdown might occur if they relinquish power; the postcolonial chaos in Angola or Mozambique offers them scanty grounds for optimism. Above all, the Europeans are aware of the sorry fate suffered by so many ethnic minorities in postcolonial situations, a fate never predicted by the Western academics who called for an end to Western empire in the name of a higher morality. The list of these minorities is a long one— the Indians in Uganda and Burma, the Arabs in Zanzibar, the French-speaking settlers in Algeria, the Kurds in Iraq—long enough to dampen the decolonizing zeal of the most ardent idealist. As far as the white South African minority is concerned, there is nothing to prevent its being exposed to expropriation in, or expulsion from, South Africa if it should lose all power.

South African society, of course, is distinguished by great differences of wealth, and world opinion considers these disparities blameworthy. This social differentiation is in no sense unique, however. The gaps in power, income, and status that divide the ruling strata from the workers in the Soviet Union and the People's Republic of China are certainly greater, but for some reason South Africa's inequalities, because they are based on race,

appear much more reprehensible. South Africans think—and indeed, discriminate—in ethnic terms. So, of course, did the Poles and the Czechs:
after World War II they enforced their own form of ethnic apartheid by
physically expelling the German minorities, irrespective of class affiliation.
So did the Ugandans who expelled their Asian minority, and the Tutsi who
slaughtered hundreds of thousands of their Hutu neighbors without incur-
ring much condemnation from the world community. The fact that all
communist regimes discriminate against people because of their class or
their political views is also largely ignored. Intellectuals seem to think that
it is only wrong to discriminate against a man because of his color, not
because of his class. There are also vast regions of the world in which people
are oppressed because of their religions, but these oppressors do not receive
the condemnation that South Africa gets.

Yet South Africa is not like most communist countries. It does not have
to build fences and walls to keep its people in, nor is it avoided by its
neighbors; something like 1.5 million Africans from Botswana, Lesotho,
Swaziland, and other countries have voted with their feet to live in South
Africa. Mozambique, a Marxist-Leninist republic, continues to send work-
men to South Africa on labor contracts. No such extensive migration occurs
to any communist country, nor, indeed, to any other African country. South
Africa does not expel ethnic or religious minorities; on the contrary, it
attracts immigrants, both white and black. By comparison with Castro's
Cuba, the People's Republic of China, or the Soviet Union, the people of
South Africa enjoy extraordinary liberties. The English-speaking press is
solidly arrayed against the government. The freedoms that churchmen or
academics enjoy in South Africa would appear unbelievable to them were
they in China, North Korea, Vietnam, or even Czechoslovakia. A reputation
as an active government supporter is an essential qualification in all universities of the Second World and many of those in the Third World. In South
Africa, on the other hand, a candidate known to back the ruling party stands
assured of having a hard time at any English-speaking university. South
Africa is judged by a set of standards very different from those applied to
communist or Third World countries. From being a trusted friend of the
Allied nations in World War II, South Africa has become a "pariah state"
not only to those countries but to the entire world.

Although the critics of South Africa differ in many respects, they agree
that the collapse of the South African regime is both historically certain and
morally just. They claim that its system depends on color privileges for a
minority and that its neofascist regime prohibits freedom of thought and
keeps the majority of its people in slavery. The urban masses are subject to
a steady process of impoverishment—if not in absolute terms, at least in comparison with the privileged whites. The so-called "Bantu homelands" are a

sham. In a more fundamental sense, the South African system imposes even more burdensome shackles on the means of production. These shackles must be smashed lest South Africa sink into stagnation. The United States should therefore align its policy with those of the Third World nations, and this it has done on numerous occasions. Paradoxically the radical state of Mozambique continues to deal extensively with South Africa.

Mozambique justifies its close relations with the republic on the grounds that it needs South Africa. While black governments in the UN demand broad economic sanctions against South Africa, Mozambique and many other African and Arab nations continue to deal with the pariah state. South Africans legally recruit Mozambican blacks to work in the gold mines of the Transvaal; the ports of Maputo and Beira are largely run by South Africans, and the goods passing through these ports are mostly South African cargo. Mozambique railroads carry South African goods, and about 40 percent of all government revenue comes from this transit trade.

While Mozambique joins in condemning apartheid in the OAU and the UN, it does not hesitate to deal with South Africa. Businessmen from South Africa get royal treatment; there are daily flights from Johannesburg to Maputo. Businesses run by South Africans have not yet been nationalized, although almost everything else has been. Hundreds of South African technicians help to keep Mozambique running. Machel's government sells South Africa electric power from the Cabora Bassa complex that South Africa helped to build and to finance. In spite of all these connections between Mozambique and South Africa, the United States will not let American naval ships dock at any South African port. If a radical state can be pragmatic about South Africa, why cannot we? Or take the case of Zambia, another African opponent of apartheid: South Africa is one of its premier trading partners, a source of much-needed mining machinery and other supplies. South Africa exports not only industrial products, but also food, a vital commodity at a time when many African states are short of victuals.

The orthodoxy of the lecture room and the political caucus therefore leaves much to be desired. In economic terms, at any rate, the development of South Africa has been an extraordinary success story. Sixty years ago South Africa was a poverty-stricken land dependent, like so many Third World countries today, on the export of raw materials. Today it is the economic giant of the continent. Its GNP is more than ten times that of Kenya and more than twenty times that of Ethiopia. It is a major producer and exporter, and the only sub-Saharan country capable of producing the most sophisticated manufacturing products—from mining machinery to computers. Its industrial growth rate has, in fact, been astounding. Between 1916 and 1970 its manufacturing output alone increased in value from 27,908,000 rands to 3,101,892,000 rands. It is the wealthiest, fastest growing, most powerful state of Africa. South Africa produces 20 percent of the continent's wealth, 40 percent of its industrial production, 80 percent of its steel, and 60 percent of its electricity, and it has 50 percent of all the automobiles and telephones in Africa. This record has occasionally been obscured by the ideological asymmetry of many Western opinion makers who are apt to condone—or try to explain—the excesses of communist regimes in Russia or China by pointing to their progressive function in promoting development while they deny a comparable alibi to South Africa's government.

The injustices and inequalities to be found in South Africa are apparent to all. There is widespread poverty in rural areas, and widespread discontent. Nevertheless, black South Africans have derived very real benefits from the progressive nature of the country's economic system. Life expectancy in western Africa is 39.2 years; in South Africa it is 50 years. Wages of blacks have gone up steadily, with their rate of increase exceeding that of white wages during the past five years by 49 percent. Social services concerned with health care, education, and similar areas still leave much to be desired, but they have expanded impressively. Nineteen percent of South Africa's black people attended school in 1971, compared with an estimated 9.7 percent in the rest of Africa, and eleven thousand blacks were enrolled in universities in 1977. Economic development and diversification have eroded traditional color-bar practices in industry. Ironically, it has been the Nationalist government, dedicated to the principles of apartheid, that has done more than any of its more liberal predecessors to develop social service for blacks. Since 1971 the government has built more than three hundred thousand houses in the black homeland areas. Between 1962 and 1975 white taxpayers in South Africa spent twice as much on development for blacks as the UN did in thirty-eight of the world's poorest countries. South Africa then should not be treated as a pariah state; it should be dealt with in the same manner as communist states or other authoritarian, nondemocratic regimes.

2
South Africa:
Strategic and Economic Potential

Cape Town was known to the early mariners as the Tavern of the Seas. It is one of the strategic prizes of the world. European settlement in Southern Africa began in 1652 with the arrival of Jan van Riebeeck, who had been sent out by the Dutch East India Company to establish a station on Table Bay, a port of call where Dutch ships might obtain fresh water and provisions on the long route to the East Indies. During the French Revolution and the Napoleonic Wars, the Cape of Good Hope passed into the hands of Great Britain and became a cornerstone in the development of British sea power. Without command of the sea-lanes around the Cape, the British position in the South Atlantic and the Indian Ocean would have been untenable, and the makers of British strategy knew this. Again in World War II, Great Britain could hardly have sustained hostilities against the Axis powers in the Middle East without command of the Cape route. When the Mediterranean was closed by the Germans, the Cape played an equally important part in the defense of Allied shipping; experts have estimated that out of five convoys of one million tons each approaching Europe in wartime, four had to round the Cape. Had German U-boats denied the use of the Cape route to Allied ships, Great Britain would certainly have been hard pressed and Nazi Germany might well have won the war. The importance of the Cape route has continued to grow since World War II.

Control of the Cape route remains a major asset to the West. An average of 6,800 ships called at South African ports each year between 1957 and 1966. The number almost doubled when the Suez Canal was closed as a result of the Arab-Israeli conflict. It reached a yearly average of about 12,000 for the period 1967 to 1972. A total of 950 ships passed the Cape route in one month of 1974 alone. By 1975 some 24,000 oceangoing vessels passed this particular "choke point" every year—about 66 a day (see table 1). Of those 24,000 vessels, 9,476 docked in South African ports, including 1,600 or so from the United Kingdom, 1,375 from Greece, 1,064 from Liberia, 590 from the Netherlands, and 382 from the United States.

The Cape is particularly important to oil tankers, whose former route to and from the Mediterranean took them through the Suez Canal. Most of these ships are now too large to go through the canal, so more than half of Europe's oil supplies—and a quarter of its food—passes round the Cape of Good Hope. Moreover, the increasing dependence of the United States on imported Middle Eastern oil has further increased the American stake in the Cape route—already the world's most crowded shipping lane; by the 1980s, according to some estimates, 60 percent of U.S. oil imports may have to be supplied via the Cape. Additionally, the United States has defense treaties with forty-three countries, forty-one of which lie overseas. Ninety-nine percent (by volume) of its overseas trade is transported by ship. Any threat to the world's sea-lanes consequently jeopardizes American national security.

TABLE 1

SHIPS PASSING THE CAPE OF GOOD HOPE IN ONE MONTH
(February 1974)

Flag	Freighters	Tankers	Total Ships	Percentage of Grand Total
United Kingdom	118	69	187	19.20
Liberian	45	84	129	13.00
Norwegian	27	45	72	7.43
Greek	61	12	73	7.53
Communist nations	105	7	112	11.55
Dutch	30	15	45	4.64
French	17	17	34	3.50
West German	37	6	43	4.43
Italian	20	10	30	3.09
United States	16	2	18	1.86
South African	—	23	23	2.37
Japanese	24	9	33	3.40
Indian	23	1	24	2.47
Spanish	1	3	4	.41
Portuguese	9	2	11	1.13
Panamanian	19	8	27	2.78
Danish	14	5	19	1.96
Swedish	8	7	15	1.55
Miscellaneous	63	8	71	7.32
Totals	637	333	970	100.00
Daily Averages	22.75	11.89	34.64	

SOURCE: South African Defence Department.

In years to come, Western Europe and Japan will probably become even more dependent on Middle Eastern oil rather than less so, as table 2 shows. Seventy percent of Western Europe's strategic materials already must come round the Cape. Since the bulk of this traffic must skirt the coasts of Africa, its steady flow depends to some extent on South Africa and South African ports (see figure 1). The Cape route is not likely to lose its present importance in relation to the Suez Canal. According to Dr. Alvin J. Cottrell, several factors work against such a shift. The repair facilities of South Africa are growing in importance. The existing glut on the world's tanker market, and the use of tankers for storage purposes, subtract from the marginal time savings that may be attained by using the shorter Suez route. The development of South African resources and industries have changed former patterns of trade, and more shipping now goes to South Africa rather than around it. South African–European trade links are being tightened by advances made in containerization, a process that will add to the size of cargo ships and present them with problems similar to those already faced by supertankers.

A key position is now held by the VLCCs (very large crude carriers—of 160,000 tons or more). These ships require costly facilities for refueling and

TABLE 2

ESTIMATED DEMAND FOR MIDDLE EASTERN OIL
(in mbd)

Year	United States	Europe	Japan
1973	3.30	12.80	4.20
1980	14.00	19.00	9.00
1985	18.00	24.00	12.00

SOURCE: Patrick Wall, ed., *The Indian Ocean and the Threat to the West* (London: Stacey International, 1975), p. 184.

TABLE 3

THE TRADE OF SOUTH AFRICA'S PORTS, 1974
(in million tons)

Port	Exports	Imports	Total
Durban	12.5	19.9	32.4
Port Elizabeth	6.7	3.1	9.8
Cape Town	3.4	5.8	9.2
East London	0.5	1.4	1.9
Total (including Namibian ports)	31.2	33.9	55.4

SOURCE: Economist Intelligence Unit, Ltd., *Interdependence in Southern Africa: Trade and Transport Links in South, Central, and East Africa* by Julian Burgess. (London, July 1976), p. 16.

enormous dry docks for repair. The new large port of Saldanha Bay, about a hundred miles north of Cape Town, was specifically planned to accommodate tanker traffic and to provide dry-dock facilities. Another major project is Richards Bay harbor, which is linked to the development of the Sishen-Saldanha iron-ore export scheme. The deep-water port at Richards Bay is designed to accommodate vessels displacing up to 152,000 tons and, eventually, those displacing 254,000 tons. As part of a major development project, the harbor is being equipped to handle bulk cargoes such as bituminous coal and anthracite. Between them, the new ports will supplement the trade of the existing ports as they are listed, in order of importance, in table 3.

By the end of 1978 about 70 percent of South African imports will be containerized, and with the new ports in operation, the present congestion of South Africa's harbors should come to an end. The country will then be

FIGURE 1

MAIN OIL MOVEMENTS BY SEA, 1973

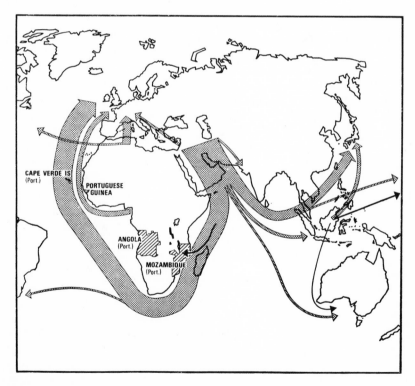

SOURCE: Institute for the Study of Conflict, *The Security of the Cape Oil Route* (London: ISC Special Report, 1974), p. 43.

in a position to dispense with the use of Maputo in Mozambique, and even to handle traffic from its various neighbors, including Swaziland, Botswana, and Rhodesia. It can also provide more technical advantages to shipping. South African engineers have developed remarkable skill in dealing with VLCCs both inside and outside harbors. Minor repairs can be made underway without slowing a vessel's speed; technicians and spare parts are transferred to and from a ship seven hours' steaming time before the vessel has rounded the Cape and seven hours after. Helicopters capable of lifting several tons can supply ships with mail, fresh food, medical help, and such. Although the VLCCs do not touch land, they depend on this umbilical cord, which can only function with a stable land base. Smaller tankers are able to use the dry docks at Durban harbor, and the deep berths in the harbors at Durban and Cape Town. At the time of writing, these ports were swamped with traffic, and lines of tankers waited to be served.

Port facilities are presently being extended to handle the oil trade and the increasing traffic in minerals and raw materials required by the West and by South Africa's expanding industrial economy. The rapidly growing demand for harbor-service vessels such as tugs, dredges, floating cranes, pilot boats, shipping craft, and naval ships has contributed to the growth of an active shipbuilding industry, fostered since 1967 by government subsidies. In 1977 South African shipyards turned out cargo vessels of a substantial size—all of direct or indirect strategic significance. These defense capabilities are augmented by a network of airfields, by a growing aircraft industry established in 1964 with the creation of the Atlas Aircraft Corporation of South Africa, and by the development of such bodies as the Council of Scientific and Industrial Research, whose Aeronautical Research Unit is concerned with high-speed aerodynamics, structures, propulsion, and aircraft operation.

As a source of strategic raw materials, South Africa is of vast importance to the Western world, as table 4 shows. Whether in peace or in war, such supplies would be hard to replace were they denied to the West. A left-wing revolutionary government in South Africa might, of course, in its own economic interest, continue to sell raw materials and to furnish maritime facilities to members of the North Atlantic Treaty Organization (NATO), but such a prospect would be problematical. The West hardly wants to rely on the fleeting goodwill of a government allied with the Soviet Union, which is itself committed to the overthrow of Western democratic governments. The prospect of dependence is grim. It is unnecessary if the United States adopts reasonable policies toward South Africa. There is no need to support radical liberation movements in South Africa; the United States should work through the country's moderates, not its militants. We want to prevent racial wars, not encourage them, and to stimulate the evolution of a stable society in South Africa.

TABLE 4

MINERAL POTENTIAL OF THE REPUBLIC OF SOUTH AFRICA

Mineral	South African Production and Reserves	Western Use
Gold	The Republic of South Africa (RSA) produces more than 70% of world's gold, and has the world's greatest reserves	World's monetary system
Diamonds	50% of the world's gem diamonds are mined in the RSA and Namibia; RSA has 50% of world's reserves and 60% of Western reserves	Gem and industrial diamonds
Coal	RSA has 2% of world's known coal reserves −12,000 million tons—and 5% of Western reserves	
Uranium	RSA produces 16% of the free world's uranium and has 25% of world's reserves and 30% of Western reserves	Nuclear power
Iron ore	RSA has vast high-quality resources; RSA possesses 6%−5,000 million tons—of known world reserves of iron ore containing 60% iron, and 8% of Western reserves	
Vanadium	RSA has world's largest known source	High-grade steel
Manganese	RSA is world's second-largest producer after USSR, has world's largest reserves of very high-quality manganese, and exports 15% of world production	Manufacture of ferro-alloys
Asbestos	RSA is sole source of crocidolite asbestos and amosite asbestos; it has 14% of world's proven reserves and 16% of Western reserves, and produces 10% of world supplies	Asbestos cement products
Chrome	RSA's production is second only to that of USSR; RSA has 25% of world's and Western reserves	Manufacture of steel
Platinum	RSA is world's largest producer and exporter; has 83% of world's reserves	Car exhaust systems, fertilizers, jewelry
Copper	RSA has one of world's highest-producing mines at Phalaborwa; holds 2% of world's and 4% of the West's reserves	Electrical and other copper products
Fluorspar	RSA has world's largest deposits; 34.6% of world's reserves	Steel production
Vermiculite	RSA has second-largest known best-quality reserves and second-highest production—39.4%—in world	Heat and sound insulation
Titanium	RSA has very large deposits; impact expected soon on world markets	Manufacture of aircraft engines and fuselages
Nickel	RSA has largest African deposits, and ranks sixth in world's reserves	Steel production
Baddeleyite (Zirconium and hafnium oxide)	Strategic mineral, at present commercially available only from RSA	Atomic reactors and special steel
Ferrochrome	RSA is largest producer in world—12.5% of world production; expected to increase	Stainless steel
Phosphate	RSA is only large producer in world, and will soon become major exporter of phosphoric acid; enormous reserves of highest quality	

TABLE 4—continued

Mineral	South African Production and Reserves	Western Use
Tin	RSA production is small—twelfth in a total list of 40 world producers, but major tin reserves are either in communist countries or in areas of relative political instability	
Lead and zinc	Recent discoveries in NW Cape could make RSA one of great Western producers	
Other	RSA: barytes, bentonite, beryllium, bismuth, calcite, corundum, feldspar, fireclay, flint clay, fluorite, fuller's earth, graphite, gypsum, kaolin, kieselguhr, lead, limestone, magnesite, mica, mineral pigment, pyrite, pyrophyllite, salt, silica, sillimanite, talc, tantalite-columbite, tantalum, tiger's-eye	
All minerals	1974 total production reached record level of 3,928 rands, including a gold production of 2,533 rands	

Source: South Africa, White Paper on Defence, 1977 (Pretoria, 1977), pp. 38–39. See also Peter Vannemann and Martin James, "The Soviet Intervention in Angola: Intentions and Implications," Strategic Review, Summer 1976, p. 96.

South Africa also forms the cornerstone of a wider system of Southern African states. South African railways, harbors, and airports play a key role in the commerce of Namibia (South-West Africa), Rhodesia, Botswana, Swaziland, and Lesotho. (Except for Namibia these are all landlocked countries that are wholly dependent on the South African communications network. Namibia alone has access to the coast, but Walvis Bay, its main port, belongs to South Africa.) South Africa's neighbors rely to a considerable extent on its capital, know-how, and technical services; they cannot do without its imports and markets. South Africa's economic influence extends even to African countries outside this state system—countries that take a militantly anti–South African stand in world diplomacy. (Zambia, for instance, has paid a heavy price for boycotting Rhodesia, yet increasing its reliance on South African supplies.)

Namibia would perish without its connection with South Africa, which supplies it with certain export markets, easy marketing facilities, price stability, and relatively high quality and low prices in imports. The South Africans also furnish Namibia with skilled manpower and a great variety of specialized services, as well as food and machinery—indeed the bulk of the country's consumer goods and physical capital. Because of its enormous natural handicaps, Namibia faces great difficulties that a poor country cannot solve on its own. It contains large areas of wasteland, its internal market is small, and its vast size makes provision of an adequate transport system expensive. All the requirements of a modern economy—cement, machinery, building materials, even food—have to be imported. Droughts are an ever-present threat. Primary industries such as agriculture, fishing, and mining— the country's basic pursuits—are vulnerable to great fluctuations in demand and to the perils posed by an unfriendly nature. South Africa, on the other hand, exports not merely machinery, but also food; its government-sponsored development schemes have started a great array of new enterprises in Namibia: bakeries, slaughterhouses, filling stations, and factories. The assistance supplied by South Africa to Namibia through the so-called Bantu Investment Corporation has been much more successful than similar foreign-aid programs mounted in Africa by Western European countries or the United States. Namibia, or for that matter Lesotho, Botswana, or the Transkei, would be ill-advised to snap the South African link. Even Mozam-bique needs South African help in a variety of fields, especially in selling its electric power and in port and railway development, as we noted earlier. South Africa attracts labor migrants from far beyond its borders, and sends capital and managers and technicians beyond its boundaries. South Africa's neighbors, then, are involved in its economic fortunes to an intimate degree. If the South African economy were to collapse as a result of internal unrest or foreign wars, the adjoining countries would suffer in equal measure.

South Africa's economic power beyond her borders is paralleled by its political influence. Countries like Swaziland and Lesotho cannot afford to alienate the South African giant. South Africa has, and for a long time will continue to have, an immense impact on the politics of Rhodesia and Namibia, no matter who rules in Salisbury or in Windhoek. Any efforts made by the West to bring peace and to liberalize the regimes of Rhodesia or Namibia will require a large measure of South African goodwill.

Conventional defense planning in the West has traditionally stressed the danger of a Soviet land assault on Western Europe. Given the weakness of the Soviet navy in the years following World War II, Western strategists were inclined to take almost for granted the existing superiority of NATO in the oceans of the world. The Suez crisis of 1956 probably helped to convince Moscow that the Soviet Union had to acquire sufficient naval strength to challenge the United States in distant parts of the globe, and the Cuban missile crisis of 1962 certainly strengthened the Kremlin's determination to turn the Soviet Union into a great maritime power. Under the brilliant leadership of Admiral Gorshkov, who was appointed commander-in-chief in 1962, the Soviet navy rapidly expanded. By 1976 the USSR possessed a nuclear-powered, submarine-launched, ballistic missile force—including sub-marines under construction—superior to the combined U.S., British, and French naval forces. The Strategic Arms Limitation Talks (SALT) agree-ment stabilized the inferiority of the United States by setting a lower ceiling for U.S. nuclear submarines than for the Soviet ones, an arrangement that would have been inconceivable at the time of the Cuban crisis.[1]

The Soviet Union's naval forces include missile cruisers, missile-firing patrol boats, destroyers, a powerful air arm, an amphibious force, and a logistics support force of tankers and supply ships that lessens the navy's dependence on foreign bases. In addition, the USSR has a great merchant fleet (which is expected to reach twenty-seven million tons in 1980), the world's largest fishing fleet (approximately four thousand vessels in 1976), and a flotilla of hydrographic survey ships that provide detailed military intelligence. Unlike Western merchant fleets, these ships are centrally controlled from Moscow; their personnel are interchangeable, and naval and civilian ships are designed for mutual support.

The goal of U.S. designers is to produce ships that are fit to exercise control of the seas over long periods—naval vessels characterized by endurance, survivability, and habitability—while Soviet planners have a different object. They stress lightweight construction permitting a high degree of maneuverability and great offensive firepower—qualities needed for a fleet whose mission is to deny control of the seas to an enemy. Soviet naval strategy in the 1970s, unlike that of the first half of the twentieth century, which was designed to defend the homeland, is geared to isolate the United States by cutting the sea lines of communication that connect the United States with its allies and its sources of raw material, and to enable the Soviet military to support "wars of liberation" around the world. This strategy was demonstrated in a worldwide context by the great "Okean '75" exercises. More than a hundred ships were deployed in coordinated operations in the North Atlantic, the Mediterranean, the western Pacific, and the Indian Ocean; Soviet aircraft operated from facilities in Cuba and Guinea among other locations.[2]

In this ongoing struggle against the West, Soviet strategists place much emphasis on the strategic importance of Africa. The "liberation" of South Africa would strengthen the military position of the Soviet Union in the world at large. "Liberation" would also put the USSR and its future allies in a position to deny vital raw materials to the Western world whenever the political situation demanded such a course. The Soviet navy would play a major part in this process. In peacetime, Soviet warships would provide backing to Soviet diplomacy. In wartime, as Admiral Gorshkov puts it, the fleet would assure "the disruption of the ocean lines of communication, the special arteries that feed [the enemy's] military and economic potentials."[3]

The power of the Soviet Union and its allies on land and in the air, make the capabilities of its navy seem even more impressive; they also make direct numerical comparison between U.S. and Soviet naval forces somewhat misleading. The transoceanic trade of the Soviet Union is small. Soviet fleets are not needed to protect Soviet shipping on the high seas. These naval forces are only justified by Soviet planning for war—to deny oceanic transit to the Western world, thereby crippling NATO, starving Europe and Japan into surrender, and isolating the United States. True naval parity therefore requires NATO forces not only to be stronger than those of the Warsaw Pact, but also to be well supplied with overseas bases at a time when the menace of Soviet submarines is infinitely greater than the threat of German U-boats was in two world wars.

Between 1969 and 1973 alone, the number of "shipdays" of Soviet warships and auxiliaries, excluding submarines, increased from 1,400 to 7,250. The strengthening of the Soviet fleet was not paralleled by a comparable Western effort. Given the vital dependence of the NATO powers on the availability of Middle Eastern oil, the South Atlantic and the Indian Ocean play a particularly important part in Soviet calculations. Since 1968 Soviet naval vessels have maintained a permanent presence in the Indian Ocean, while the NATO alliance has not been operating there or in the South Atlantic. The USSR, moreover, gained a variety of naval and air facilities in such diverse locations as Hodeida in Yemen and Umm Quasr in Iraq, among others.

These strongholds are not necessarily secure. During the Somali-Ethiopian war that started in 1977, the Soviets lost their Somali facilities, having shifted their support to Ethiopia. With Soviet and Cuban help Somalia has been defeated. If Ethiopia should succeed in restoring its power in the rebellious province of Eritrea the Soviet position might be enormously strengthened. As a reward for the services rendered to Ethiopia by Cuban troops and Soviet advisers, the Soviet Union might acquire a naval base at Massawa. This port may be valuable not merely as a threat to Western communications, but also as a means whereby the Soviet Union could help to safeguard its own maritime route to the Soviet Far East.

The United States, which has also sent task forces to the Indian Ocean, would like to freeze both its own naval presence in the Indian Ocean and that of the Soviet Union at their present levels. President Carter made the demilitarization of the Indian Ocean a campaign issue in 1976. Agreement is not likely to be reached, however, given the extent of Soviet reservations. The Soviets, moreover, continue their support to "wars of national liberation" in Rhodesia, Namibia, and South Africa that are directed against Western interests, while insisting on the universal illegitimacy of Western support for all anticommunist movements. The Soviets have begun a military buildup in Mozambique and are stockpiling supplies. By April 1978, 250 tanks and 35 MIG-21 fighters and SAM missiles were spotted at Maputo. Whatever happens, the Soviet Union's use of its political influence, naval power, and intelligence skills, added to its existing and potential facilities for naval deployment, continue to make the USSR a powerful force in the Indian Ocean.

The Kremlin's position in South Africa has been further strengthened by the Soviet-Cuban conquest of Angola and by Soviet support for Mozambique; both of these nations are self-proclaimed Marxist-Leninist republics. In the past, the maritime facilities in Portuguese Africa were open to the United States. Thus, when the Suez Canal was closed as a result of the Arab-Israeli war of 1967, Luanda in Angola and Lourenço Marques (now Maputo) in Mozambique became key ports in relation to U.S. naval deployment in the South Atlantic. In rotating ships of the U.S. Middle East force "home-ported" at Bahrein in the Persian Gulf, for example, an American destroyer had to sail from its naval base on the east coast of the United States back across the Atlantic to Monrovia in Liberia, where it replenished and then proceeded to Luanda for new supplies. From there the destroyer had to embark on the longest, most treacherous part of its journey—twenty-eight hundred miles around the Cape of Good Hope to Maputo. This long trip was necessary because, for political reasons, the U.S. navy is unable to use any of the excellent ports available in South Africa (seè figure 2).

The trip was dangerous for a destroyer; by the time the vessel had reached Maputo it was well below 25 percent of its fuel capacity. A vessel low on fuel is less stable than one that is fully loaded, and bad weather encountered on rounding the Cape endangers crew and ship. Today, in 1978, the ports of Angola and Mozambique are no longer available to the U.S. navy. The U.S. installations on the island of Diego Garcia in the Indian Ocean are much further to the north and east, but Diego Garcia is not suited to be a major naval base.

Nuclear-powered vessels, of course, are much less dependent on foreign bases than are conventionally powered ships, but a substantial portion of the U.S. fleet continues to require conventional fuels. Nonnuclear attack carriers of the seventy-thousand- to eighty-thousand-ton class such as the *John F. Kennedy*, for instance, must still round the Cape, and they require replenishment at sea from supply ships and oilers at planned intervals along the route.[4] In fact, the U.S. navy's capability to replenish its ships at sea gives it a mobility and endurance for sustained operation the Soviet navy cannot yet match.

America's loss has been Russia's gain. At the time of writing, Mozambique still enjoyed some degree of independence from its Soviet and Cuban allies, but Soviet influence there was on the increase. East Germans supposedly controlled the country's vast security apparatus, which was designed to cope with widespread internal protest against the despotic rule of the National Front for the Liberation of Mozambique (FRELIMO). Soviet and Cuban advisers trained the country's armed forces. Above all, the Soviets were reported to be turning the deep-water port of Nacala into a naval base to give themselves a major stronghold in the southern part of the Indian Ocean.[5]

The Popular Movement for the Liberation of Angola (MPLA) regime in Angola, for its part, depended on Cuba and the Soviet Union for its very existence. Cubans controlled the administration and the secret police. An estimated army of twenty thousand Cuban soldiers helped the government

FIGURE 2

THE NAVAL BALANCE, UNITED STATES–USSR, 1977

WORLD'S MARITIME CHOKE POINTS

1. Straits of Florida
2. Windward Passage
3. Mona Passage
4. Iceland Strait
5. Iceland Strait
6. Barents Strait
7. Persian Gulf
8. Red Sea
9. Strait of Gibraltar
10. Danish Straits
11. Mozambique Channel
12. Strait of Malacca
13. Tsushima (Korea) Strait
14. Cape of Good Hope
15. Suez Canal
16. Panama Canal

Shaded areas on figure above are Soviet footholds.

THE NAVAL BALANCE

Units	United States	USSR
Major Combat Ships	177	200
Submarines	117	380
Carriers	13	2

Reprinted with permission from Captain Paul B. Ryan, USN Retired, "Canal Diplomacy and U.S. Strategic Interests," *Naval Institute Proceedings*, (January 1977).

forces to cope with widespread resistance on the part of guerrillas operating in both northern and southern Angola. The Cuban ambassador, Oscar Oramas, one of the architects of Cuba's invasion of Angola and a senior figure in the Cuban communist party, was a key operative of the DGI (the Cuban intelligence service), which in turn is supervised by the KGB. The Soviet Union has made no attempt to secure naval bases in Angola, but this position could well change. It is possible that the USSR—or conceivably even other Warsaw Pact powers like East Germany—would seek strategic gains by developing facilities in the deep-water ports of Lobita Bay and Luanda. Baia dos Tigres in southern Angola has a superb deep-water anchorage that, if properly developed, would provide an excellent harbor for Soviet submarines preying in wartime upon the busy maritime African coast. Modern airfields at Luanda and Lobito, and at Henrique de Carvalho in central Angola, could be enlarged to accommodate long-range aircraft.[6] Should Cuban and Soviet forces therefore strengthen their foothold in Angola and Mozambique, the position of the Western nations would further deteriorate.

The South African naval and air forces are in no position to deal with the Soviet menace on their own. Still, they are technically proficient, and their potential is being augmented. South Africa's most important naval base, situated in Simonstown, one of the most important naval positions in the southern hemisphere, is being expanded at a cost of fifteen million rands. When planned operations are completed—possibly by 1981—Simonstown will accommodate between forty and fifty additional naval vessels, and will have tripled its 1977 capacity. The South African navy commands additional bases at Walvis Bay in Namibia and at Durban. Naval and air reconnaissance are centered on Silver Mine in the Cape Peninsula in bombproof underground installations that have been deeply tunneled into rock, and naval headquarters were shifted in 1977 from Silver Mine to Pretoria, where they coordinate closely with the army and air-force commands. Silver Mine provides central direction for detailed surveillance of the maritime routes of the southern hemisphere. If South Africa were to form alliances with other nations, Silver Mine would be capable of accommodating representatives of their naval forces.

The South African navy itself is primarily designed to cope with danger from submarines and mines, and to provide coastal defense (see table 5). The South African naval forces were designed for cooperating with Western navies in safeguarding the Cape route. The imposition of a Western arms boycott has since prevented South Africans from purchasing additional warships in the West. They now concentrate on shore defense and emphasize the construction of home-built, missile-carrying speed boats. The South African navy patrols the littoral and the local approaches of the republic and of

Namibia. Continuous daily air reconnaissance provides essential information concerning shipping—including Soviet shipping—round the Cape, while helicopters provide South African frigates with a stand-off weapons delivery system. The South Africans could, therefore, give valuable support to any Western force operating in the Indian Ocean. Above all, Simonstown offers a complex overhaul, repair, dry-dock, and storage capability that is unequalled elsewhere in the Indian Ocean and comparable in sophistication only to Singapore. Diego Garcia, which is being developed as a permanent support base to provide logistic assistance to U.S. carrier forces, will be only a fueling station with a modest replenishment capability. As noted previously, for political reasons, the United States has abstained from the use of South African naval facilities and from cooperation with the South African naval command.[7]

TABLE 5

SOUTH AFRICAN NAVY AND AIR FORCE, 1977

Branch	Strength and Equipment[a]
Navy:	5,000 men, including 1,400 conscripts
	3 Daphne-class submarines
	2 destroyers with 2 Wasp ASW helicopters
	5 ASW frigates: 3 with 1 Wasp helicopter each
	1 escort minesweeper (training ship)
	10 coastal minesweepers
	5 patrol craft (ex-British Ford-class)
	On order: 2 Agosta-class submarines
	2 Type A69 frigates
	3 FPBG
	6 corvettes with Gabriel II SSM
Reserves:	10,500 men in Citizen Force
	1 frigate
	7 minesweepers
Air Force:	8,500 men, including 3,000 conscripts
	133 combat aircraft
	2 light-bomber squadrons with 6 Canberra B(1)12, 3 T4, and 9 Buccaneer S50
	3 FGA squadrons with 16 Mirage IIIEZ and 14 IIIDZ
	1 FGA squadron with 15 F-86 (being replaced by Mirage F1AZ)
	1 fighter/recce squadron with 27 Mirage IIICZ/BZ/RZ
	1 interceptor squadron with 16 Mirage F1CZ
	2 MR squadrons with 7 Shackleton MR3, and 20 Piaggio P166S Albatross
	4 transport squadrons with 7 C-130B, 9 Transall C-160Z, 23 C-47, 5 DC-4, 1 Viscount 781, 4 HS-125, 7 Swearingen Merlin III
	4 helicopter squadrons, 2 with 40 Alouette III, 1 with 25 SA-330 Puma and 1 with 15 SA-321L Super Frelon
	1 flight of 12 Wasp (naval-assigned)
	2 comms and liaison squadrons (army-assigned) with 23 Cessna 185A/D/E, 36 AM-3 Bosbok, 3 C-4M Kudu

SOURCE: International Institute for Strategic Studies, *The Military Balance 1976–77* (London, 1976), p. 45.

[a] The figures given may underestimate the actual strength of the South African forces, which is given in table 8.

3

The Defense Infrastructure

With the publication in 1947 of *When Smuts Goes*, which outlined South Africa's impending breakdown, Arthur Keppel-Jones started a new genre of futurology. Many scholars and journalists over the last two decades have predicted the collapse of white-controlled South Africa by internal revolution, external intervention, or a combination of the two. These assumptions require a reassessment based on military and economic facts, taking into account South Africa's strong economic and political position. It is the only sub-Saharan state with an industrial and logistic infrastructure strong enough to enable it to maintain by itself a reasonably up-to-date system of land, air, and sea defenses. South Africa, on its own, can field a balanced force, with a modern navy, an air arm, and an army complete with armored formations.

The country's military policy is based on the assumptions that threats to South Africa are not merely local, that a bipolar conflict continues in the world, and that the Kremlin will continue to proclaim the need for intensifying the international class struggle between "socialism" and "capitalism." The nuclear balance of terror has made the threat of conventional war greater rather than smaller. Peace is indivisible because every local conflict affects to some degree the global balance of power. South Africa's military preparations aim, therefore, at providing for counterinsurgency warfare of short and long duration, and for conventional war-making ability. The country's striking power is based on part-time forces, with specialist leadership provided by a strong permanent nucleus.[1] Strategic doctrine stresses the need for effective intelligence, the ability of the defense force to support the civilian administration at a moment's notice, the maintenance of a mobile force available for immediate duty, and the need for decisive action and for "total defense" that embraces every aspect of national power.

South Africa's president, who is elected by a bicameral parliament, is nominally commander-in-chief of the South African Defence Force (SADF). Effective power is vested in the prime minister who, to all intents and purposes, controls the defense forces through the ministry of defense. In addition, the ministry of justice, police, and prisons (set up in 1966 as the ministry of police) has functions linked to internal defense. South Africa reputedly maintains an extensive internal and external intelligence network that has sources not merely within South Africa, but also apparently within states of the Organization of African Unity (OAU), the Warsaw Pact, and Western Europe. Intelligence data are collected and evaluated by the Bureau for State Security (BOSS), an independent governmental department that directly advises the prime minister on questions affecting internal and external security. National security is coordinated by a State Security Council (SSC), which advises the prime minister on the formulation of national strategy, including its political, economic, psychological, and military aspects. All of these intelligence groups are dynamic and interacting.

South Africa, as we have indicated, is the industrial giant of the African continent, the only African country with a major iron and steel industry and with petrochemical and advanced engineering plants. The republic's military power is thus enhanced by a substantial industrial and logistic infrastructure on a scale that has been attained nowhere else in Africa. The defense establishment is linked to great quasi-governmental bodies such as the South African Iron and Steel Industrial Organisation (ISCOR, created in 1928), the Nuclear Fuels Corporation, the Uranium Corporation, and the South African Coal, Oil, and Gas Corporation (SASOL, set up in 1957). The country produces iron, steel, chemicals, and a broad range of high-grade engineering goods, all of which have military significance. Its nuclear technology is of a high order, and South African scientists have developed their own method of enriching uranium that will multiply the nation's earnings from foreign trade. South Africa expects to become a large exporter of uranium within about ten years. This may bring it increasing political influence, as experts expect serious worldwide shortages of both raw and enriched uranium during that period.

South Africa also has the technology required to build nuclear weapons.[2] Until now it has abstained from testing nuclear bombs, but it has not signed the nuclear nonproliferation treaty. This places U.S. diplomats in a difficult position. The United States has continually urged South Africa to sign the treaty. According to Joseph Nye, Jr., a deputy undersecretary of state and architect of President Carter's nuclear policy, the United States would be willing to sign security agreements with future signatories of the nonproliferation treaty, offering U.S. nuclear guarantees as a substitute for nuclear weapons, in addition to the benefits of nuclear cooperation in the civil sphere.

Since South Africa already possesses its own nuclear energy, and since the Carter administration could not possibly offer a military guarantee to South Africa, the benefits of signing the nuclear nonproliferation treaty are by no means apparent to South Africans. Their nation, already one of the world's nuclear powers, will certainly further strengthen its international position in that field.

The defense complex, including ARMSCOR (which was created in 1976 through a merger of the Armaments Board and the Armaments Development and Production Corporation of South Africa) with its subsidiary arms factories, is one of the country's most advanced technical organizations, one that is engaged in manufacturing, operating, and maintaining a wide range of highly sophisticated equipment. About 45 percent of defense expenditures goes to internal development, providing private industry with a considerable work load and spreading technical know-how to the entire labor market, particularly to the engineering profession.

A major effort has been made to maintain adequate oil reserves. The extent of these is not known, but by 1977 the country was reputed to have stored a two- to five-year oil supply in abandoned mine shafts. Coal liquefaction has been perfected through SASOL for the purpose of producing fuels, petrochemicals, fertilizers, and tar products. When present plans are completed, South Africa will supposedly produce about 36 percent of its fuel needs from domestic sources.[3]

Defense and defense-related industries thus have considerable impact on the South African economy (see table 6). Defense expenditures have risen considerably during the past seven years—from about 2.3 percent of the GNP in 1969–1970 to an estimated 5.3 percent in 1977–1978.[4] Despite the increase, South Africa's expenditures have not been excessive in comparison with those of countries like the United States, Nigeria, or the USSR. Though they are a burden on the economy, defense expenditures do not cause a major political or economic strain, given the extent of the country's resources.

South Africa's industrial infrastructure enabled the country to emphasize self-sufficiency in arms production and improvement in its ability to withstand foreign economic pressure, especially pressure applied through an oil boycott. Arms production has recently been centralized through ARMSCOR. According to a ministerial statement issued in 1977, South Africa supplied 75 percent of its arms requirements, excluding naval craft, from domestic sources. By 1977 weapons manufactured at home included missiles, electronic equipment, motorized equipment like the Ratel infantry combat vehicle, small arms, maritime assault vessels, naval frigates, and ordnance. Before joining the international arms embargo, France had supplied the country with submarines and other naval craft. Jordan, oddly enough, had furnished it with tanks, and Israel had sold it naval craft and expertise. A variety of aircraft were being produced under French and Italian licenses, including Mirage fighters, the SA 330 Puma helicopter, and the MB-326M Impala light-strike aircraft.[5] The key nation involved in building up the South African arms-manufacturing potential was France: Panhard provided

TABLE 6

SOUTH AFRICAN DEFENSE EXPENDITURES, 1975–1978
(in million rands)

Expense	1975/76	1976/77	1977/78
Command and control			
Operating costs	76.6	92.9	112.8
Capital costs	23.7	32.1	62.2
Total	100.3	125.0	175.0
Landward defense			
Operating costs	223.3	283.3	424.9
Capital costs	238.6	361.7	482.2
Total	461.9	645.0	907.1
Air defense			
Operating costs	20.5	25.5	79.6
Capital costs	42.5	46.3	46.1
Total	63.0	71.8	125.7
Maritime defense			
Operating costs	26.3	31.5	33.3
Capital costs	59.6	130.7	198.8
Total	85.9	162.2	232.1
General training			
Operating costs	53.1	43.0	61.9
Capital costs	11.3	28.8	6.3
Total	64.4	71.8	68.2
Logistic support			
Operating costs	154.5	218.7	250.8
Capital costs	83.6	78.3	137.5
Total	238.1	297.0	388.3
Personnel support			
Operating costs	11.5	10.9	16.7
Capital costs	15.7	20.2	22.7
Total	27.2	31.1	39.4
General SADF support			
Operating costs	2.7	3.7	4.6
Total defense requirements			
Operating costs	568.5	709.5	984.6
Capital costs	475.0	698.1	955.8
Total	1,043.5	1,407.6	1,940.4
Cash voted (all departments)	1,043.5	1,407.6	1,711.7
Estimated percentage of state expenditures	15.0	17.0	19.0
Estimated percentage of GNP	4.1	4.9	5.1

SOURCE: South Africa, *White Paper on Defence, 1977* (Pretoria, 1977).

licenses for armored cars; the Société nationale industrielle aérospatiale and its subsidiary, SUD Aviation, helped to provide equipment to manufacture the Mirage; and French firms sold helicopters and submarines and other military hardware to South Africa (see tables 7 and 8).

According to testimony introduced by Sean Gervasi to the Subcommittee on Africa of the U.S. House Committee on International Relations, the South African arms build-up is considerably greater than has been indicated by conventional sources such as the London International Institute of Strategic Studies or the *Defense and Foreign Affairs Handbook* (see table 9). Thus South Africa is in a position to deploy substantial armored forces supported by a modern and well-trained air force. The South Africans have not as yet tested nuclear weapons, but they have the industrial capacity, the technical knowledge, and the raw materials required to construct a substantial nuclear arsenal and a tactical delivery system. The country's military power is therefore greater than at any other time in its history.

South Africa's defensive capability is likely to be affected to some degree by the international arms boycott that was recently imposed on the country by the UN. The nation produces all the matériel required for counter-insurgency warfare, but it still requires foreign skills in complex forms of

TABLE 7

DELIVERIES OF WEAPONS SYSTEMS KNOWN TO BE IN SERVICE WITH THE
SOUTH AFRICAN DEFENSE FORCES (BY THE END OF 1976)

Item	Manufactured/ Licensed By	Numbers Delivered	IISS[a]
Mirage III fighter/bomber trainer/recce	France	95+	57
Mirage F-1 all-weather multipurpose fighter	France	48+	16
Aermacchi MB-326M Impala I strike/trainer	S.A./Italy	300	145
Aermacchi MB-326K Impala II strike	S.A./Italy	100	22
Aerospatiale Alouette III armed attack helicopter	France	115+	40
Aerospatiale/Westland 330 Puma assault helicopter	France/U.K.	40+	25
Centurion Mk 7 heavy tank	U.K.	150	141
Daimler Ferret Mk 2 scout car/antitank armored car	U.K.	450	230
M-3A1 White armored personnel carrier	U.S.	400	n.s.[b]
Saracen FV603 and FV610 armored personnel carrier	U.K.	700	n.s.
T-17 El Staghound armored car	U.S.	450	n.s.

SOURCE: Sean Gervasi, testimony to U.S. Congress, House, Committee on International Relations, Subcommittee on Africa, July 1977.
[a] International Institute for Strategic Studies, *The Military Balance 1976–1977* (London, 1976).
[b] Not specified.

military engineering connected with rocketry, computers, and nuclear arms. The decision made by the French government at the end of 1977 to halt the construction and trial run of the *Good Hope*, a warship being built for South Africa, was an ill omen, but the South Africans will certainly surmount the boycott, just as the Rhodesians have done with far fewer resources. South Africa's industrial strength, its ability to pay for imports in gold, and the nature of international trading "leaks" have rendered the country largely immune to formal boycotts. It is difficult, therefore, to dissent from the considered opinion of the *Washington Post* that the arms boycott has come too late:

> Compared to any of the Black African countries on or near its borders, South Africa has a huge arsenal and a military expertise that is far superior to any of them now or in the near future. The Soviet Union is involved in arming Angola and Mozambique, but neither is likely to pose even a potential threat to the South Africans for years, and probably decades.[6]

TABLE 8

DELIVERIES OF WEAPONS SYSTEMS NOT GENERALLY KNOWN TO BE IN SERVICE
WITH THE SOUTH AFRICAN DEFENSE FORCES (BY THE END OF 1976)

Item	Manufactured/ Licensed By	Delivered
Lockheed F-104G Starfighter/bomber	U.S. ex-Luftwaffe	40
North American F-51D Cavalier c. insurgency strike	U.S.	50
Aerospatiale/Westland 341 Gazelle general-purpose helicopter	France/U.K.	2(?)
Agusta-Bell 205A Iroquois utility/s.r. helicopter	U.S.	25
Lockheed P-2 Neptune antisubmarine patrol	U.S.	12
Centurion Mk 10 heavy tank	U.K.	240
M-47 Patton main battle tank	U.S./Italy	100
M-41 Walker Bulldog light tank	U.S.	100
AMK-13 light tank	France	80
M-113A1 armored personnel carrier	U.S./Italy	(400)[a]
Commando V-150 armored personnel carrier	U.S./Portugal	(300)
Piranha armored personnel carrier	Switzerland	(100)
Shorland Mk 3 armored car	U.K.	(200)
Short SB 301 armored personnel carrier[b]	U.K.	(300)
Sexton 25 pdr self-propelled gun	Canada	200
M-7 105 mm self-propelled gun	U.S.	200
M-109 155 mm self-propelled gun	U.S./Italy	(50)

SOURCE: Sean Gervasi, testimony to U.S. Congress, House, Committee on International Relations, Subcommittee on Africa, July 1977.

[a] Figures in parentheses indicate orders on which delivery continues.

[b] In service with the South African Police.

The Defence Force of South Africa operates as an integrated organization under the chief of the defense forces, assisted by the respective chiefs of staff of the army, navy, and air force. The so-called Defence Planning Committee consists of the combat force commanders, the senior federal manager of ARMSCOR, and a number of special members appointed by the minister. The Defence Staff contains divisions for operations, personnel, intelligence, logistics, and management service. Further modifications of the army structure have been made to assure rapid local control of counterinsurgency operations, and the Defence Force has completed a number of major telecommunications projects that are regarded as its nerve center.

The army's peacetime strength by 1978 was officially estimated at 41,000 men, including 34,000 conscripts; there were 8,500 men in the air force, 5,500 in the navy, and 90,000 in the commandos, a paramilitary force designed for local defense and counterinsurgency operations. The number of soldiers actually mobilized in 1977 may have been considerably larger—some observers place their full strength at about 130,000 men. If necessary, South Africa could mobilize 250,000 members of the Citizen Force and, by calling up all reserves, between 400,000 and 450,000 men. The backbone of the Defence Force is the Permanent Force of professional cadres; its flesh and bones, so to speak, are the reservists of the Citizen Force, who provide the bulk of the combat and administrative units that would be deployed in the field if the republic were at war. Like the commandos, reservists serve for a year and are then called up annually for short training periods during the subsequent five years. They can be quickly mobilized for service and, after a brief and intensive period of retraining, can be committed to full-scale operations. Their morale is high, and postings to the border areas of

TABLE 9

ARMS INVENTORY: SOUTH AFRICAN DEFENSE FORCES (BY THE END OF 1976)

Item	IISS[a]	Currently in Service
Combat aircraft	113	625
Helicopters	92	215
Tanks	161	525
Armored cars	1,050	1,430
Armored personnel carriers	250	960
Self-propelled guns	n.a.[b]	294
Medium and light artillery	n.a.	380

SOURCE: Sean Gervasi, "The breakdown of the arms embargo against South Africa," testimony to the U.S. Congress, House, Committee on International Relations, Subcommittee on Africa, 14 July 1977.
[a] International Institute for Strategic Studies, The Military Balance, 1976–1977 (London, 1976).
[b] Not available.

Rhodesia, Angola, and Mozambique sharpen their training through experience in field operations.

There are eleven territorial commands in the armed forces, each with its own training units and full-time force units. Similar Citizen Force units are readily available to combine with Permanent Force units into brigades and task forces. By 1978 these were officially listed as an armored and a mechanized brigade (with Centurion tanks), four motorized infantry brigades, two parachute battalions, and seventeen artillery and antiaircraft artillery regiments, along with engineer, signal, and other specialist troops. According to Gervasi's testimony, before the House subcommittee, the South Africans have accumulated armored vehicles and personnel carriers of many different designs, and an impressive force of helicopters (see tables 7, 8, and 9).

The land forces are supported by a balanced air force consisting of a six-squadron strike force, a four-squadron maritime command, a four-squadron air transport command, and a light-aircraft command that includes helicopters and light fixed-wing aircraft. The need is emphasized for mobility, decentralized control, close cooperation between land, sea, and air forces, cooperation with the civilian population, and close acquaintance with local terrain—both in conventional and in counterinsurgency warfare. Air defense is strengthened by static and mobile radar units, coupled with modern interceptors and backed by surface-to-air missiles. The Defence Force resembles that of Israel in that its strength depends essentially on the reservists.[7]

The career cadres of the Defence Force, the Permanent Force, make up only 7 percent of the entire defense establishment and less than 3 percent of the land forces. The Permanent Force is small in relation to the tasks assigned it, and South African military experts constantly complain of personnel shortages. The Defence Force has no trouble attracting recruits; its difficulty lies in keeping trained men. The steady turnover works against the cost-effective deployment of experienced manpower. The services of these highly trained men are not entirely lost, however, as they automatically join the reserves and can be called up by the Defence Force in case of need.

The Permanent Force, which was once mainly a preserve of English speakers, is now primarily officered by Afrikaners. According to figures published in the Johannesburg *Star* on 13 December 1974, some 85 percent of the Permanent Force staff in the army and 75 percent of the corresponding staff in the air force consisted of Afrikaners. The South African navy, however, still retained a large number of English-speaking staff—about 50 percent—and was still jokingly referred to as the "Royal South African Navy."[8] Promotion in the military goes by merit rather than by linguistic affinity, although Afrikaans dominates the soldiers' mess. The officer corps does not form a separate caste; its ethos is technocratic, as befits a cohesive white society devoid of feudal traditions. Its members are better educated than they were in the nineteenth century, when locally raised units were comprised of a large number of frontiersmen trained in the bush rather than at school. Today officer candidates are required to pass the matriculation examination, and subsequently receive an advanced military education. Possibly one-third of all officers are former sergeants. The creation of the Military Academy of the South African Defence Force in 1950 further contributed to military professionalization in an army whose officers rarely had degrees. Today the officer corps is one of the country's many professional groups; it is not a military caste but an integral part of the professional middle class.

The architects of the military academy wanted to place officers' training on an equal footing with the training of professional men in civilian jobs in order to raise South African military standards to those attained overseas by equipping officers to cope with an increasingly complicated defense structure, to service sophisticated weapons, and to carry out military and related research. The academy was originally affiliated with the University of Pretoria; later its staff became the faculty of military science, military history, geography, and such, but also taught subjects like mathematics, political science, public administration, aeronautics, nautical science, accountancy, computer science, and physics. Graduates initially advanced into the lower and middle echelons of the Defence Force; by the 1970s they were being promoted into top-ranking posts.

The South African Defence Force reflects the strengths and weaknesses of the country's white society at large. It contains a high proportion of men with developed technical skills. South Africans can thus maintain and deploy sophisticated modern equipment much more easily than can most of the black African forces whose recruits are drawn mainly from the villages. The army is essentially the white electorate in arms, so the country does not face military coups d'état of the black African and Latin American varieties. The army is highly motivated, and is integrated into European society. Desertion and major infractions of discipline are not great problems. "Fragging" is unknown. South Africa is exempt from the class conflict that divided America during the Vietnamese war, when a large stratum of college students —mostly of middle-class origin, exempt from the draft, and often guilt-ridden about their status in society—were arrayed against resentful blue-collar workers who were being conscripted into the army. The common military experience by whites of all social ranks and language groups strengthens cohesion in a country where white reservists feel that they are defending their own homes rather than some distant colony.

The armed forces are nonpolitical in the sense that their members are not expected to belong to a particular party. If they have any political leanings, they tend to be more pragmatic about them than the older Afrikaner establishment and the police; the latter are regarded by critics as the "mailed fist of apartheid." The army has rarely been used for police duty, and it enjoys greater popularity than the police. The public appeal of the fighting services is enhanced by their excellent record in combat. South African troops did well in the two world wars, and also in recent operations in Angola where—contrary to Cuban propaganda—they more than held their own against Cuban troops. South Africa's withdrawal from Angola was caused by logistic and supply problems and by the lack of U.S. support; it was not caused by Cuban forces.

The army, like major industries, is also more pragmatic in racial affairs than the older South African establishment. Admiral H. H. Biermann, chief of the South African Defence Force until 1976, felt convinced that South Africa must be able to call on all races for defense if it were to be able to resist the potential Soviet threat in the South Atlantic. His successor, General M. A. de M. Malan, shares Biermann's view. The South African navy recruits Coloured and Indian as well as white sailors. In 1975 the Defence Force began to accept recruits for a recently created Cape Corps Service Battalion composed of Coloured citizen soldiers; they are eligible to join the Permanent Force at the expiration of their twelve-month training period. In the same year, for the first time in the history of the South African Defence Force, Coloured soldiers received commissions.

In addition, the South Africans began to recruit a limited number of Africans; by the time of writing, the first black battalion was being constituted, and plans were under way for providing the black homelands with small forces of their own. Judging by the Rhodesian precedent, South Africans seem likely in the future to rely more extensively on African and Coloured fighting men, a development fraught with wider social consequences.

For purposes of "internal defense," South Africa places considerable trust in its police force, which was established in 1913 by amalgamating the four provincial forces. Unlike the British or American police, that of South Africa is a national force. It is a semimilitary body, and is regarded as the "first line of defence in the event of internal unrest"; its members receive a thorough training in infantry drill, infantry combat, and the more conventional police skills. Its administrator, known as the commissioner of the South Africa police, is responsible to the minister of police. (The commissioner's duties are extensive since in addition to conventional defense and police responsibilities, policemen are expected to undertake inquiries on behalf of government departments; in the more remote country areas they also act as assistant clerks and court messengers, and as immigration officers, wardens, revenue and census officers, health inspectors, inspectors of vehicles, postal agents, meteorological observers, mortuary attendants, and more.)

By 1975 the police included about 54,000 men; 68 percent of these were whites (mostly Afrikaners), about 28 percent were Africans, and the balance consisted of Indians and Coloureds.[9] The official goal is to permit each segment of the population to be policed by members of its own community. Contrary to the prevailing stereotype, South Africa is not a "police state" in the sense that the streets are full of policemen on the beat. The total number of policemen per thousand people stood at 1.42 in 1912; sixty years later the figure is almost the same—1.48. The proportion of policemen to civilians in South Africa is smaller than it is in the United States; moreover, public order has been maintained in South Africa with relatively little violence. Albie Sachs, a bitter critic of apartheid, has estimated than between 1917 and 1973 South African policemen have opened fire on rioting crowds on roughly thirty occasions (including Sharpesville in 1960), killing five hundred Africans in all. He considers that his estimate may be on the low side; another three thousand Africans may have lost their lives during the same period when individual policemen opened fire—allegedly while hunting suspects or in self-defense.

For Sachs, these figures indicate a long-continued reign of white terror. Certainly, thirty-five hundred people slain are thirty-five hundred too many, but in comparison with European countries like Germany and Russia over a sixty-year period, or with many African countries that have attained independence since World War II, South Africa has been extremely pacific. Zambia, for instance, has in many ways been a model African state—a country that has avoided savage civil war of the Nigerian kind, or ethnic mass slaughter of the sort that decimated postindependence Burundi. Yet in Zambia, more than seven hundred people were killed in one year alone— 1964—when the Zambian government smashed the so-called Lumpa Church, a dissident ecclesiastical organization.[10]

The practice of measuring South Africa with a different set of weights derives not from the real nature of South Africa's misdeeds but from the country's relative liberality. In South Africa, foreign journalists and foreign academicians can move about the country and report with much greater freedom than they can, say, in Mozambique or Angola. Police brutalities are publicly investigated and commented upon in parliament, in the press, and in academia. Government-appointed commissions of inquiry (such as the so-called Theron Commission appointed in 1973 to investigate the condition of the Coloureds) provide evidence of abuses at public expense. Such facilities do not exist in Marxist-Leninist republics like Angola or Mozambique, or even in so-called bourgeois states like Zaïre. South Africa thereby gets a disproportionate amount of unfavorable publicity of a kind that reflects the easy accessibility of the evidence more than its nature.

Contrary to a wide-spread stereotype, the average white South African policeman is not necessarily brutal, ill educated, or inefficient. European recruits must have at least a "junior school certificate," and must be fully bilingual; special training is available at police training colleges—one for each major racial grouping—with advanced courses at the University of South Africa for officers who seek academic qualifications (including a B.Pol. degree).

Nevertheless the police force has many weaknesses. Policemen are not particularly well paid. And, as Jordan K. Ngubane, a South African writer, explained in his testimony given before the U.S. Senate, the bulk of the police are compelled to perform a great deal of unproductive labor. Much of their work deals with the enforcement of apartheid legislation, giving them the kind of unpopularity the armed forces have avoided. African policemen are more poorly educated than whites; black recruits are accepted with a "standard 6"—that is, an elementary-school background. Black South Africa is actually underpoliced; fifteen thousand black police are too few to enforce the law among a population of some nineteen million black people in an area larger than Western Europe.

There is a serious crime problem in major cities like Cape Town and Johannesburg. Neverthless, the police should not be underestimated. Life and property are safer in the white areas in South African cities than in most American urban communities of comparable size; the police can take some credit for this accomplishment in a racially diverse country that is riddled by differences of class and income. With the support of an extensive intelligence network, and with the supervisory powers entailed in the various pass laws and in antiterrorist and anticommunist legislation, the police form a vital component of South Africa's internal defense. They are trained to act in cooperation with the armed services and the civil administration, and are well equipped for the task of counterinsurgency. No revolutionary breakdown could occur without being preceded by an effective disruption of the police establishment.

4
South Africa:
A Revolutionary Situation?

How stable, then, is this establishment? To what degree is it subject to revolutionary change? Can the system be overthrown by military action or by naval blockade? Alternatively, will the South African establishment succumb to revolution from within, to guerrilla warfare, to urban terror, or to more peaceful movements such as demonstrations and strikes that could culminate in the breakup of civil authority?

Conventional War against South Africa

War games are an exercise in futurology, and like all futurological exercises they usually bear little resemblance to what actually happens. The number of variables is too large and the field of knowledge is too small to make accurate predictions possible. Military planners, like their colleagues in the social sciences, can only make educated guesses, but some guesses are more accurate than others. We believe that a number of possible scenarios may, without question, be discarded from the start.

Combined action on the part of the Organization of African Unity may be excluded. On paper, the independent black states of Africa can raise considerable forces. In 1977 the Nigerian armed forces amounted to some 221,000 men, organized in four infantry divisions, twelve independent regiments, and supporting units; the army of Zaïre, organized into thirty battalions, numbered 34,400 men. The members of the OAU, however, lack a common military organization, military doctrine, leadership, training methods, deployment plan, and general staff. Armies like those of Zaïre, for logistic reasons, cannot operate in strength outside their own borders, and they have yet to prove that they can fight a modern, Western-style army.

The value of possible future support to African insurgents from the OAU states, however, is admittedly not to be discounted.[1] These nations could supply weapons and training, and military bases on the borders of South Africa. But the African states could hardly send their own armies against South Africa. Such an operation would endanger the stability of army-centered states such as Zaïre or Nigeria, whose armed forces are essential to the strength of the existing governments. The Zambian army is small; it includes some five thousand men organized into four infantry battalions with their supporting units. Angola is unusual among the African states in seeking to build a people's army based on conscription, but it has been ravaged by civil war, and its equilibrium depends on the presence of foreign troops.[2] Mozambique offers no offensive threat to South Africa other than that of harboring guerrillas, although a recent Soviet weapons buildup should be noted.

Intervention by means of conventional forces thus would have to be carried out with troops drawn from outside Africa, possibly with "proxy armies" supported by the Soviet Union. Their employment is not inconceivable. Soviet and also East German theoreticians defend the despatch of Cuban soldiers to Angola as a new form of "international working-class solidarity." The Cuban example might well be followed by others. Cuba itself is not in a position to launch yet another large military campaign overseas; its total armed strength in 1978 was only 189,000 men and more than a fifth of them were heavily engaged in Africa. Even a more powerful state like East Germany, whose armed peacetime forces number 201,000 men including security units, could not contemplate a major effort outside Europe (although minor ventures might be possible).

Assuming that members of the Warsaw Pact were willing to risk armed action in South Africa, and assuming that they were able to overcome the political obstacles in their way, they would still face extraordinary difficulties. An army determined to invade South Africa by land would lack suitable bases. In 1978 Mozambique could hardly have served as an advance base for a great army because of the country's economic dependence on South Africa. Cuban and Soviet advisers have come to Mozambique in substantial numbers. Despite FRELIMO's socialist and anti–South African rhetoric, however, Mozambique miners continued to work on the Rand, hydroelectric power from Mozambique was still sold to South African industries, and South Africans were running the port of Maputo. Mozambique, moreover, is deficient in communications, especially in traffic links from north to south. Only one bridge crosses the Zambezi; all other crossings are by ferry. Mozambique harbors are inadequate, with Beira poorly dredged and available only for coastal shipping, while the larger port of Maputo—like Beira—has a channel approach. In 1978 the Soviet navy used the port of Nacala, which is too distant from South Africa to form as yet a serious threat.

Angola is even less likely than Mozambique to menace South Africa. The country was in a perilous condition by 1978. European settlers had departed, leaving the country without most of its managerial and technical skill; the coffee crops had largely failed; UNITA, a dissident southern group, remained active; traffic had not been restored on the Benguela railway; and in many parts of Angola the Cubans and MPLA government forces controlled only the towns. North–south communications were totally inadequate. The logistic problems alone eliminated Angola as a possible base for an army operating against South Africa. Namibia is equally ill suited to become a base for hostile action, even if it were to become an independent country beyond South African control. Its coastline is desolate and poorly supplied with ports. The terrain is mostly inhospitable; the distances are vast. South African armored forces could easily strike at the flanks and rear of invading units as they advanced inland.

Rhodesia (Zimbabwe) would be better suited to become a land base, should the country move into the communist orbit. It is well supplied with roads, airfields, and railway communications, and it has substantial industries that would afford supply and repair facilities to an enemy army. An invading force striking southward from Rhodesia, however, would still encounter enormous obstacles. Inland communications routes are long; the Limpopo River is a natural barrier, and the bridges across it could easily be knocked out. In any case, the Soviet Union would be hard pressed to provide the transport required for building up a land-borne invasion force that would have to operate against a strong enemy on the other side of the world. This opponent, moreover, would enjoy all the advantages of internal lines of communication and mobile defense, resting on a powerful industrial infrastructure. The sheer extent of South Africa's territory (471,000 square miles) would enable it to rely on defense in depth.

The defending armies might well be hampered by guerrilla operations (as we show in the following section), but partisan operations in South Africa have so far been negligible. Even were they to increase in extent, they could not be mounted on a scale that would prevent South African forces from operating effectively. Comparable situations are numerous. During World War II Soviet partisan formations rendered superb service. They functioned in a country where the Nazis had alienated most of the population by insane atrocities. Swamps, forests, and sometimes mountainous country offered excellent hideouts. Considerable stocks of weapons were available; so was assistance from the Soviet High Command. Yet the ability of the guerrillas to interfere with German military operations still remained strictly limited.

They could never prévent the German army from striking where it wished. The position of potential guerrilla forces in South Africa would be much more difficult; such forces would be in no position to equal—much less improve on—the past performance of Soviet guerrillas.

A seaborne invasion might be considered as an alternative to an assault by land, always assuming that the South Africans had no nuclear weapons to prevent such a venture from the start. In 1965 the Carnegie Endowment for International Peace prepared a contingency plan. Its report, entitled *Apartheid and United Nations Collective Measures*, envisaged naval and air operations that might ultimately culminate in a full-scale invasion of South Africa—a venture that would require at least a hundred thousand UN soldiers and would entail casualties ranging from nineteen thousand to thirty-eight thousand men. As fighting continued, the blacks in South Africa would step up their own campaign of violence and terror, the South African Defence Force would lose control over the internal situation, and the regime would collapse. The South African army is now a great deal stronger than it was in 1965, however. An invading force of a hundred thousand men would surely be inadequate today. Even if the political difficulties preventing UN action could be solved, the black resistance groups would lack both the arms and the organization to play the part assigned to them by the Carnegie Endowment planners.

A South African "D Day" would be a more difficult undertaking under present circumstances than the series of landings in North Africa and even in Normandy in World War II. An invading force capable of smashing South African resistance would require considerable numerical superiority over the defenders; no less, perhaps, than three armored divisions, three mechanized divisions, and two airborne divisions, with extensive technical and logistic support and decisive air superiority, would be required. The effort to maintain such a force would be staggering. South Africa has a limited number of ports, and they are relatively easy to defend. An invader would have no adequate bases—with harbor, supply, and repair facilities—available within several thousand miles of the Cape. A seaborne force would have to be marshalled in distant cities like Rio de Janeiro or Dakar, with an advance base in Luanda.

The invaders would also have to overcome logistic difficulties. An allied army landing at Cape Town would still be a long way from the Pretoria-Johannesburg complex, South Africa's industrial heartland. Landing at Durban would add to the length of seaborne supply lines. The Durban harbor could be blocked without difficulty, and the heavy surf on the beaches south of Durban would make the use of landing craft particularly perilous. Having occupied South Africa, the victor would presumably have to administer and feed a disorganized civilian population whose supply system would probably have broken down. The political consequences of an invasion would be hard to predict. Only one thing can be said with certainty: a defeated and disorganized South Africa would not be governed by a liberal and democratic regime of the kind favored by liberal academicians responsible for the Carnegie war plan. Defeat in war, unless it is followed by a long and effective military occupation, is apt to produce chaos or armed dictatorship. The chances of establishing a liberal, pro-Western regime in South Africa as a result of armed intervention are nil. The chaos and bloodshed of Angola are a more likely result.

The project would also encounter extraordinary political difficulties. The airlift, amphibious, and engineering capabilities, together with the tremendous concentration of power, needed to execute such an operation are presently commanded only by the United States. The South Africans are convinced that the Americans will not wage such a war in Southern Africa; from the standpoint of U.S. political, strategic, and economic interests such an enterprise would indeed be sheer lunacy.

A naval blockade of South Africa might be considered a less bloody way of forcing the country to its knees. Conceivably, the UN might—at some future date—call upon the Soviet Union and its allies to blockade South African ports until South Africa agreed to dismantle its political system. The Soviet Union might perhaps accept such an assignment, given the right political atmosphere. The Soviets might even offer to work in collaboration with U.S. naval forces as part of an international campaign against "racism"—a campaign that would revert to the principles of the Popular Front on a global basis. International intervention could even draw on past precedents, such as the actions taken by the Great Powers against the "Unspeakable Turk" in the nineteenth century or by the British African Squadron against slave traders.

A blockade would also entail intervention on the part of nuclear-powered vessels that were not dependent on local supplies of fuel. A blockade of South Africa would hardly affect the economy of the Warsaw Pact states; the West would be injured much more severely and Western Europe, especially Great Britain, would be affected much more seriously than the United States. A blockade would interfere with facilities for the vital tanker traffic round the Cape, and would deprive the Western nations of their commerce and their returns from South African investments.[3] The countries most seriously affected by a blockade would be backward, vulnerable states like Mozambique, Malawi, Zambia, Lesotho, Botswana, and Swaziland that have economic ties with South Africa.

South Africa would also suffer severely. Fuel consumption would be drastically cut. Industrial production would diminish. Farming would suffer. Unemployment would increase. Living standards would fall, particularly among the Africans, who would be less able to defend their economic interests than the whites. A blockade would not by itself, however, bring about the overthrow of the regime. The country would be reduced to a siege economy that could strengthen the existing state machinery by extending its armory of economic controls (such as rationing). South Africa is sufficiently well supplied with raw materials and industrial and scientific resources to withstand a siege. The country's only major deficiency is oil, but its dependence on imports of such essential materials is being curtailed through oil hoarding on a huge scale and through the expansion of its coal-to-oil production. In some respects South Africa might even benefit from the challenge of a blockade by being compelled to further diversify its economic production.[1] For Western interests as a whole, however, a blockade of South Africa would constitute yet another political and military defeat.

Prospects for a Violent Revolution

South Africa has a revolutionary tradition, albeit one that is very different from the left-wing stereotype. In 1899 it fought a civil war against British overlordship. In 1914 an Afrikaner minority that was opposed to South Africa's entry into World War I took up arms. Eight years later the country was once more in the throes of an attempted revolution; white miners on the Witwatersrand went into battle in an uprising designed to protect white living standards. Their slogan, "Workers of the world unite for a white South Africa," strangely blended racist with communist sentiments. The rebels were organized into well-armed commandos. They enjoyed a certain measure of sympathy from Afrikaner reservists in the Union Defence Force who were drawn—like the strikers—from the ranks of poverty-stricken white countrymen. According to a secret report issued by the South African Defence Headquarters at the time, the rising was extremely dangerous and might well have overpowered Union forces had similar insurrections broken out in other urban centers.

The movement failed, but the skilled European workers were henceforth accepted into a political partnership with the ruling establishment; as a result, the promised South African revolution receded into the future. The insurrectionary forces had failed because they had not been able to secure substantial white support. They had been denied the backing of white skilled workers, technicians, foremen, and industrial supervisors—a group indispensable to the success of a city-born revolutionary movement. From a national perspective, the Afrikaner people—once a semiproletarian community containing most of South Africa's "poor whites"—ceased to be a revolutionary element. The European working class made its peace with the establishment in return for substantial economic concessions. By World War II the "poor whites" had largely been absorbed into industry and service occupations. Unemployment, once the bane of white workers, ceased to be a major problem for the European workers.

The long-promised "coming revolution" will have to depend primarily on people of African, Coloured, and Indian origin. But, as we have indicated, these groups are split along ethnic and cultural lines. The Indians have little or nothing to gain from an African victory; it would place them in the same exposed position as their fellows in East Africa, where Indians have been expelled or have suffered racial discrimination. Militant intellectuals apart, Indians, Coloureds, and Africans do not identify strongly with one another. The theoreticians of "black consciousness" look to a united antiwhite front of all oppressed, whether they are brown or black; but studies on social attitudes between the races have provided little evidence for the growth of a collective antiwhite consciousness among educated Coloureds and Africans.[5]

The leadership of the militant opposition has suffered from serious structural weaknesses that in turn reflect the country's social structure. Political leadership has traditionally depended on white intellectuals and professional people. (According to a widespread stereotype, these have been either Jews or British South Africans, with an occasional Afrikaner thrown in, but actually Afrikaners have played a major role in the opposition—for instance "Bram" Fischer, a leading communist; Piet Beyleveld, an advocate of Coloured rights; and Jan Steytler, a distinguished Progressive.) The opposition, however, has failed to recruit Afrikaners into the revolutionary ranks, and this has been a serious disability in a country where previous attempts at both armed insurrection (in 1914 and 1922) and extended guerrilla war (during the South African war, 1899–1902) depended on Afrikaners. African, Indian, and Coloured leadership has lacked a strong industrial base; the militant cadres have derived mainly from the ranks of clerks, teachers, lawyers, clergymen, and journalists and from the industrial periphery—men ill suited either to run or to wreck an industrial economy.[6]

Recent changes in the composition of the industrial labor force have somewhat improved the position of the revolutionaries. Africans now occupy an increasing number of skilled and even submanagerial positions. Nevertheless, the establishment remains strong. Managerial positions in industry have not been infiltrated, nor have leading posts in the civil service, the fighting forces, and the police. Revolutionaries cannot aspire gradually to occupy leadership posts within the arms industry, the petrochemical industry, the iron and steel industries, telecommunications, aviation, the merchant marine, and other such enterprises. Therefore they cannot easily disrupt the country's essential industries or take over the economy in the event of a successful revolution.

The opposition is divided and poorly organized. The most far-reaching claims for the allegiance of all South African revolutionaries come from the Communist Party of South Africa (SACP), founded in 1921, and the oldest Marxist-Leninist party on the African continent. An orthodox pro-Marxist party, SACP was banned in South Africa in 1950. It operates mainly in exile, with its center in London, and it tries to operate underground in South Africa as well. SACP works in alliance with associated "mass organizations" like the South African Congress of Trade Unions (SACTU), the South African Indian Congress (SAIC), and the South African National Congress (ANC). The ANC is another exile organization; founded in 1912, it was banned in 1960. Once purely nationalist in orientation, the ANC is now indistinguishable in outlook from SACP, although it claims to hold to the Freedom Charter. The ANC is allied to the Zimbabwe African Peoples Organization (ZAPU), a Rhodesian exile organization that is now part of the so-called "Patriotic Front." SACP also has links with SWAPO. These bodies, like FRELIMO and MPLA, describe themselves as "movements" or "fronts"; in other words, they do not claim to be disciplined parties, but profess to unite "the masses" under Marxist leadership.

A number of advantages accrue to SACP. More than any other Marxist-Leninist party in Africa, it draws its support from gifted intellectuals, most of them exiled; many of these people (such as Ruth First and Brian Bunting) have become prominent in academia and have had their works published overseas. SACP and its allies also draw organizational and financial support from the Eastern Bloc. Through their publications SACP and the ANC can thus create abroad an image of great strength that is not warranted by their real numbers and influence. *African Communist*, a quarterly published by SACP in London and printed in East Germany, holds an important position ideologically. The party is linked to a network of overseas antiapartheid organizations—not necessarily Marxist—that are supported by liberals, humanitarians, moderate socialists, and communists who collaborate in the tradition of the Popular Front against what they regard as a fascist and racist regime. SACP exercises varying degrees of influence in some of these organizations through the classic method of getting party members into key positions. (The Anti-Apartheid Movement in Great Britain seldom diverges from established SACP orthodoxies, while the ANC closely cooperates with the World Peace Council, a Soviet front organization.)

The exiles' morale has gained vastly from the success of Mozambique and Angola in attaining independence, from the growing respectability accorded to Marxist-Leninist revolutionaries in the West, and from optimistic expectations concerning the future of Rhodesia and Namibia. Nevertheless, the opposition suffers from serious problems. The exiles are often out of touch with their own country; they are subject to severe internal quarrels; they (rightly) fear the activities of South African agents in their midst; and they are excessively optimistic about the chances of a quick change in their political fortunes. These are weaknesses that have been common to exiles throughout the ages. The opposition also has other deficiencies. Formal leadership within the SACP has fallen to elderly people—to men like Moses Kotane, an African veteran and the SACP secretary-general, and Dr. Yusuf M. Dadoo, the party's Indian chairman and the successor to J. B. Marks, who died at an advanced age in 1971. The party does not publish details concerning its middle-level leadership. It relies heavily, however, on a group of men and women now in their early fifties who live abroad. (Prominent left-wing militants include Lionel and Hilda Bernstein, Brian Bunting, Fred Carneson, Joe Slovo, Ruth First (Slovo), and others.) From the African standpoint, the SACP suffers from a major deficiency: the leading expatriates are mainly white intellectuals in an army of officers without soldiers. The SACP has not tried to maintain a united front with other exiled groups, such as the Unity Movement of South Africa. The latter condemns SACP on the grounds that "its preponderant element . . . is drawn from the White petty bourgeois intellectual section" who have "their own Herrenvolk prejudices."[7] Another dissident body that at is odds with SACP is the PAC (Pan-Africanist Congress of Azania [South Africa]), which was founded in 1959 by P. Leballo and the late R. Sobukwe as a breakaway movement from the ANC. The PAC censures the ANC, and also SACP, for their reliance on white leadership, their links with Moscow, and their divorce from the African masses. It, too, was banned in 1960. The PAC admires the People's Republic of China, while SACP takes the Soviet Union for its model.

On the question of how revolution is to be accomplished, the resistance movements are equally divided. The PAC has an almost anarcho-syndicalist vision of a spontaneous rising in which the masses will take to arms and sweep away an impotent white regime. Inspired by the Chinese example, the congress looks toward insurrections in the cities that will pin down the enemy's forces from the outset. These risings, supported by widespread African strikes, will in turn provide the opportunity for guerrilla warfare in the countryside. The African struggle will be prolonged. Still the insurgents will have to rely on their own efforts alone, not on UN intervention.[8]

For its part, SACP considers that the coming guerrilla struggle must be initiated in the rural areas, and must be coordinated with armed efforts in the cities. Armed combat, while necessary, should not be considered purely from the military standpoint, but must be conducted by "political cadres, subordinate to the political movement," with operations "planned to arouse and organize the masses."[9] SACP does not view the impending confrontation as merely a local matter. South Africa occupies a key position within the worldwide capitalist system. The victories of the MPLA and FRELIMO in the former Portuguese colonies have opened a new chapter in the history of revolution. To use the party's jargon, they have introduced "a truly qualitative change" and opened up gigantic new perspectives, "the possibilities of which are breathtaking."[10] Nevertheless, SACP argues, the revolution will not arrive at the tip of Russian or Cuban bayonets, but only by a united effort of all vanguard movements. The party thus looks to united action with bodies such as the South African Student Organisation (SASO) and the Black People's Convention (BCP, now also banned). SACP welcomes the growth of the black-consciousness movement, while criticizing the "go it alone" philosophy of young black militants who are suspicious of white and Indian allies. It remains opposed both to exclusive forms of black nationalism and to "separate development." In SACP's view, the African "homelands" have no future. Their inhabitants can never be more than white puppets. In practice, therefore, SACP ignores their very existence, thereby forgetting the Leninist principle that revolutionaries should operate through any institution that actually commands some degree of power.

SACP and its allies, in other words, wield little real power. Their importance has been vastly exaggerated by a curious conjunction of forces—the propaganda of SACP and its Soviet and pro-Soviet backers abroad, and the publicity given to the party by the South African government at home. The party and the South African government, each for its own purposes, have a vested interest in magnifying SACP's assumed influence, but the party's real revolutionary potential is negligible at present. The tales spread by white propagandists and red agitprops alike concerning an impending Marxist revolution in South Africa should be consigned to the realm of political fable, where they belong.

Nonviolent and Semiviolent Ways to Revolution

There are many ways to start a revolution. Not all of them require mounting the barricades. Some theoreticians believe that a regime weakened from within and lacking support from the people at large might succumb to a combination of civil disobedience and strikes. In theory, the notion sounds attractive; in practice, the aim is hard to achieve in a country whose governing cadres are quite solid. In South Africa the theory was first tested during the 1950s, when the ANC launched a series of passive-resistance campaigns. The ANC hoped that these campaigns would gather irresistible momentum and would overstrain the resources of the government; hence the government would be forced to surrender. South Africa's resources, however, proved vastly superior to those available to the ANC. In the end, "the structure of Congress and its inability to create a firm communications network capable of learning by its errors served to make Congress action self-defeating, despite its great potential of support among Africans in South Africa."[11]

Civil disobedience has been tried in other ways. Africans have attempted at various times to oppose the government by tearing up their passes, burning down the huts of "collaborators" in rural areas, and boycotting buses. Failures have been universally rationalized on the grounds that such campaigns helped to "educate the masses." In fact, such ventures have never had any lasting impact on the power structure except in the imaginations of their planners.

Industrial strikes have also been widely considered as a political weapon. Their use is by no means new in South Africa. In 1920, for instance, some forty thousand African mine workers went on strike in an industrial disturbance that was much more extensive than those that affected South Africa during the 1960s. The strike weapon was blunted to some extent by South Africa's reliance on migrant labor (which is hard to organize) and by the influx of labor from abroad—from countries such as Mozambique, Botswana, and Transkei where wage rates are lower than they are in South Africa. Industrial action would become more effective if South Africa were to be denied the services of these labor migrants. The mine industry cannot easily do without foreign labor; only a minority (albeit an increasing one), of South African mine workers come from within the borders of the republic. The majority are from Lesotho and the Transkei; some also come in from Botswana and Mozambique. The coal-mining industry could exist without outside labor, but the gold mines could hardly function, since they cannot be mechanized as easily as open-cast mining.

Industrial action in South Africa, however, faces formidable obstacles. Even if the Transkei were to develop sufficiently to be able to stop exporting its labor, Lesotho would continue to send its sons abroad. The South African labor force is ethnically split. Whites and blacks do not cooperate easily; neither do the Zulu, the Sotho, the Tswana, and other black ethnic groups. There are striking contrasts between skilled and unskilled, between white-collar and blue-collar workers, and above all between workers with jobs and the unemployed.[12] These conflicts do not make the strike weapon irrelevant, however. More Africans are entering the industrial labor force. More Africans are gaining skilled and responsible positions. There are now many opportunities for successful strikes that aim at improving the workers' income and conditions. Black trade unions, which are legal, though they are denied official recognition at present, are certain to increase their bargaining power in the future.

Industrial action, however, cannot easily be turned into an insurrectionary weapon. At present the black labor force in South Africa is too isolated politically, too heterogeneous in character, too poorly organized, and too unstable occupationally to stage the equivalent of, for example, the British general strike of 1926. The former British High Commission Territories, the countries along South Africa's northern rim, and the Bantustans within the country's own borders presently provide the country with a great reserve army of migrant labor. Until this army has been "demobilized," the strike organizer's task will remain immensely difficult. Even if these obstacles were to be surmounted, strikes could hardly be used as a means of overthrowing the government. Foreign precedents for the use of strikes as a means of political warfare, compared with economic pressure, have not been encouraging. The British general strike of 1926 was a failure. The millions of foreign workers employed in Nazi Germany during World War II could never even attempt to disorganize the German war machine.

The same objections apply to the use of riots and sabotage. Soweto, the huge black suburb serving Johannesburg, was shaken by bitter riots in June 1976, and by more violence throughout 1977. Some six hundred people were killed in the 1976 riots. Rioters burned and looted in protest against government policies. The riots made effective administration of the huge township, with its 1.2 million people, infinitely difficult, and worsened relations between the government and the population. Militant students managed to persuade or coerce nearly two hundred thousand students in Soweto schools to boycott classes and the idea caught on; but school boycotts, however impressive, do not affect the basic power structure. In the long run, they merely limit the education obtained by the students, thus making their struggle for a good job even harder than it was in the first place. Since Soweto is more than fifteen miles outside Johannesburg, its riots had little direct impact on the whites, and threatened neither projects nor businesses.

The riots threw into sharp relief the internal conflicts between young people and their elders, between men with jobs and the unemployed, between workers and students. They also gave expression to widespread African discontent.[13] Resentment is prevalent against the government's pass laws, against control of entry into the cities, against the operation of the color bar, against a multitude of restrictions great and small, against discriminatory forms of education, against the police, and against an ever-expanding bureaucracy. The riots led to a number of administrative reforms. For instance, the South African authorities promised that Soweto would be granted full autonomy in local government. The riots, however, did not succeed in setting off a serious urban insurrection comparable to the white miners' rising in 1922; hence the country's basic structure was left unaltered.

Many of South Africa's critics simply refused to accept the inability of the rioters to change the basic structure of government. The riots supposedly expressed a new black consciousness that was bound to transform South Africa. Sooner or later, these critics believed, white morale would crack and

South Africa would become ungovernable. They seemed to be oblivious to the fact that similar predictions had been made for a generation; every riot, every commotion had, at the time, supposedly presaged similar consequences. Over the last generation, the oppositional literature in South Africa has built up a dream world of its own, a world where time was forever "running out," where the clock perpetually marked "five minutes before midnight," where the consciousness of the oppressed eternally experienced new changes of a qualitative kind.

Nevertheless, the realities of power were very different. Even the SACP, though convinced that the riots marked a new revolutionary chapter, was cautious in its analysis:

   a. Despite the difficulties experienced by the enemy's law enforcement agencies in a few of the townships, the enemy and the organs of the state power were not in such a state of collapse or disruption that the capacity of the ruling class to act cohesively and to contain military actions, had been broken. The actions of a revolutionary movement, however well-organized, are not sufficient *on their own* to create a classical revolutionary situation. This, as Lenin has said, comes about through the maturing of special objective and subjective factors.

   b. The actions themselves although widely spread were neither altogether nation-wide in character nor did they involve the mass of the rural people. In two of the major urban centres, those around Johannesburg and Cape Town, the workers responded in large numbers, but primarily as an act of solidarity, without raising any independent demands on the issue of state power. The relatively weak response from the countryside reflects a very low level of rural liberation organization. In the towns, too, the limited response in many areas (Natal, Eastern Cape and the OFS [Orange Free State] were relatively quiet) suggests an urgent need to improve levels of political and economic organization, and of mobilization, especially at the point of production.

   c. The people remain unarmed, and this fact obviously reduces the possibility of transforming the demonstration into an effective assault on state power.

   d. The political general strike has a prime place in our revolutionary tactics. It is, however, fallacious to believe that, in the absence of general insurrectionary conditions, the working class can be expected to "starve" the ruling class into political submission by protracted withdrawal of labour. We remain convinced that in the appropriate conditions, generalized industrial action will be one of the most decisive factors in the struggle for people's power.[14]

This caution was well justified. As Engels remarked of European cities at the end of the last century, conditions for urban insurrection have become militarily less favorable than they were in the past. Since the Nationalist government took over in 1948, South Africa has seen the greatest slum-clearance program in its history. Slums like Sophiatown have disappeared. Black townships are physically segregated; they are located miles away from white cities, and government forces can regulate their access routes, electricity, and water supplies. The slum-clearance projects have not only improved housing conditions, but have also given a military advantage to government forces. Most of the African population lives in small houses laid out along straight roads that can be controlled by armored cars and helicopters, and there are few urban jungles such as those of Algeria, where guerrillas can seek hideouts in a maze of alleys, backyards, and winding lanes. A huge urban aggregation like Soweto provides some cover, but not a secure one. Soweto provides an excellent setting for the urban riot, which has traditionally been the weapon of the unemployed, the uprooted, the unpolitical looter, and the politicized young. Historically, however, riots alone have not proved to be effective means of crushing a determined government. Unarmed or poorly armed rioters cannot seize the means of production or of governance, as the widespread but wholly unsuccessful outbreaks in 1953 in East Germany showed. The police in South Africa are permitted to use firearms in case of need, and they do so. The white population at large is plentifully supplied with weapons; hence riots cannot easily spill from the black into the white areas. The courts, the legislature, and the mass media do not provide convenient sounding boards for violent protests.

Violent outbreaks may in fact strengthen government control by cementing white unity across class lines. Commotions that are confined to the African townships are likely to destroy only public facilities set aside for the use of Africans; hence violence may have the unanticipated result of opening new rifts within the black population. The aftermath of new riots may create a mood of despondency once the initial euphoria has passed and the government has had yet another opportunity to display its might. The government crackdown after Sharpeville in 1960 largely broke overt African opposition to the regime. This time black consciousness and the discontent of the youth may sustain the opposition; far more blacks are in school now than in 1961, and a mood of political inactivity may well follow in 1979. But reports from South Africa show that overt resistance has stopped in Soweto—the students are back in school.

Most important, the blacks lack a united political leadership. There is, indeed, a good deal of discontent. Many urban Africans are restless and insecure. Crime is rife in the black townships. Jobs are hard to get and to keep. The cost of living, moreover, keeps rising, and inflation always strikes hardest at the poor. Militants cannot easily get arms, however, and the masses are unwilling to rise at the sound of the clarion, for the price of failure is too high and the chance of success too small. As urban African leaders emerge they are arrested, detained, banned, or driven into exile and their movements suppressed. No single African, Indian, or Coloured leader or group has been able seriously to challenge the government and survive to operate internally. Through its use of preventive arrests and police informers the government has been able to remove or to neutralize every opposition movement to date. Youth leaders since 1976 have faced the same problem. There can be no growth of leadership if it is constantly changing. The government's pass system puts enormous obstacles in the way of organizing a national movement, and there are no signs that these difficulties are close to resolution.

The Future of Guerrilla Warfare

According to would-be revolutionaries, the surest way to victory in South Africa is through guerrilla warfare. Guerrilla warfare has become a subject of popular debate. Many revolutionary intellectuals now look to this kind of combat as the answer to all revolutionary problems—as a means of radicalizing the masses. Guerrilla warfare has acquired an aura of romance that once was reserved for the exploits of cowboys in the Far West. Yet the annals of guerrilla warfare are full of failures as well as successes. It is neither a romantic nor a new tactic, nor is it an infallible recipe for success.[15]

There are a number of well-defined routes that guerrillas have successfully taken in the past. The incumbent power, weakened by war and disillusioned in its mission, may battle for possession of a transmaritime province and finally give up, unwilling to face continued internal opposition, foreign disapproval, and vast expenditures. Such was the case of Great Britain in Ireland after World War I, and of France in Indochina and Algeria after World War II. In both cases, public opinion in the métropole proved decisive in creating a climate for withdrawal. Progressives now believe that London and New York can somehow be transformed into South Africa's métropole—a métropole that can secure the surrender of its colonial or neocolonial "possession" by financial, diplomatic, or military pressure on its satraps in Pretoria. This model, however, has no application to South Africa—hence the progressives' baffled indignation and their suspicion that a good cause is being betrayed by evil men. Alternatively, guerrillas can win if they are supported by an effective regular army. Wellington's British army in Spain rendered indispensable assistance to Spanish guerrillas fighting the armies of Napoleon. The Red Army liberated Belgrade in World War II, thereby helping Tito's forces to win. North Vietnamese regular forces redeemed the weaknesses of communist guerrilla fighters in South Vietnam and finally won the war. In South Africa, however, the guerrillas cannot mobilize regular forces of the kind that Mao Tse-tung considered indispensable to victory in guerrilla warfare.

The Portuguese experience was rather different. In Portuguese Africa the government forces were themselves radicalized by the experience of the guerrilla war. The Portuguese colonial empire collapsed—not because the army was defeated, but because its Portuguese officer corps became disillusioned with the war, overthrew the Lisbon government, and, in the case of Mozambique, actually helped to install a FRELIMO government against the efforts of FRELIMO's local white and black opponents. The South African army, however, does not suffer from the class and status divisions that plagued the Portuguese army; the South African armed forces are local bodies, not metropolitan ones. South Africans would be fighting at home, not overseas, and for their own survival, not for other people's property. Their armed forces represent the more youthful part of the white electorate; they may well act as a liberalizing element within the body politic, but hardly as a means of overthrowing the government.

The chances for guerrilla warfare are equally good in a society whose ruling class is divided, dispirited, or corrupt, as was apparently the case in Vietnam. From the partisans' standpoint, the ruling class should be incapable of further developing the country's resources; political institutions that sustain the government should have degenerated to such an extent that they serve as brakes on economic expansion. The coercive machinery of the state —the army and the police—should be easily penetrable by the revolutionaries; better still, the military forces should have suffered crushing defeat in a foreign war. The opposition should be united, and be guided by a determined and cohesive party.

None of these conditions exists in South Africa. The most radical European dissidents are to be found mainly in the churches and universities; their professional aspirations and styles of life in themselves prevent them from penetrating the army, the administration, and the police. The state machinery is efficient. The ruling groups are confident. Part of this confidence derives from the extraordinary growth in the country's economic potential, as we have noted elsewhere. Above all, the revolutionaries have no working model of an African society that is capable of appealing even to a powerful minority within the European community. Neither in civil liberties nor in economic development have the records of independent African countries like Equatorial Guinea, Uganda, Zaïre, Mozambique, or Angola been such as to inspire confidence among the whites.

Guerrilla organizers in South Africa presently face a vast array of administrative obstacles. The security forces are watchful and reasonably well informed. The police force, with its intelligence network, is more efficient and better remunerated than its opposite number in prerevolutionary societies such as late–nineteenth-century Russia. The government exercises numerous administrative restraints upon any revolutionary body; for instance, both pass legislation and the registration book that must be carried by all Africans make it difficult for them to move around the country and to organize the masses. Revolutionaries have no means of disrupting the army, either by military defeat or by subverting its morale; yet this task is one they must carry out if they are to be guided by history. It was military defeat or demoralization that provided the impetus for the English revolution of 1640, the Russian Revolution of 1917, the German revolution of 1918, and the Portuguese revolution of 1974. The revolutionaries in South Africa do not understand how to weaken the white civilian cadres. Neither black militants nor their white allies in churches and universities know how to speak the language of white workers, farmers, or businessmen. Members of the left-wing intelligentsia, commonly a diploma-bearing salariat dependent on public employment, are apt to treat workers and businessmen with the snobbish disdain that Jane Austen's gentlemen and gentlewomen once felt for persons engaged in "trade." In practice, the intellectuals' assumptions and terminology may unwittingly serve a counterrevolutionary purpose in South Africa.

Nevertheless, South Africa's rulers must take partisan power seriously. The most powerful guerrilla movement in Southern Africa at present is the Patriotic Front in Rhodesia. It contains members of both ZANU (Zimbabwe African National Union) and ZAPU. ZAPU is allied with SWAPO and the ANC, the latter being the least numerous and the least active of the three movements. Representatives of all three bodies receive training in Eastern Europe and the Soviet Union. Their arms come from several sources, with the Soviet Union as the chief supplier; weapons used in Rhodesia include the AK 47 assault rifle, the Tokarov pistol, the DSHK M 38/46 multipurpose heavy machine gun, the RPG antitank bazooka, and the PMD land mine. Rhodesia forms an exposed salient; its defenders have to guard a huge border that skirts Mozambique, Botswana, and Zambia. The northern border of Namibia is also long, but is patrolled more easily than that of Rhodesia. South Africa, on the other hand, has so far largely been shielded from assault. A guerrilla attack in strength against South Africa would face a host of technical problems.

Guerrillas have tried to penetrate South Africa through Botswana, with the Zambezi crossing point to Kazungula serving as a "freedom ferry." Botswana, however, is itself in an exposed position. Economically dependent on South Africa, geographically enfolded by Rhodesia, South Africa, and Namibia, Botswana has to tread carefully. The South Africans have strengthened frontier-control checkpoints, tightened the laws on travel documentation, increased border patrols, and assigned a fleet of motorboats to operate on the Zambezi along the Caprivi strip. Partisans who are under the command of SWAPO and depend heavily on Ovambo support are in action on the northern border of Namibia, but their military impact has been small. The level of "incidents" declined sharply during 1977; most casualties were caused by mines rather than small-arms fire. At the time of writing, SWAPO was reported to have only a few hundred men in the field; it depended on bases in Angola, where although its relations with the MPLA were cordial, the rulers could give it little help. SWAPO was hardly in a position to make serious headway against the powerful concentration of South African troops in the northern part of Namibia. Even if those troops were to surrender their present position there, topographical factors alone would render a large-scale partisan assault on South Africa from that location extremely difficult.

Similar considerations apply to partisan attacks from Mozambique. A large part of the border is covered by Kruger National Park, a vast depopulated area that provides South Africa with a buffer zone. The most vulnerable section of the border lies in the area that abuts on Swaziland and Natal. Guerrillas would surely try to use these regions as "ports of entry" into South Africa, preventing government forces from sealing off all borders. The country's physical size, however, would pose enormous logistic problems for the guerrillas, while government forces could rely on an excellent system of roads and airfields. Furthermore, the border with Mozambique has been cleared of trees and shrubs to the depth of a mile, and this cleared area has been mined, lighted, and patrolled. Guerrillas might conceivably try to counter some of these obstacles by sending sabotage teams into South Africa as labor migrants. Infiltration, however, must overcome the ever-present threat from informers, and the fact that registration books and pass laws greatly restrict the ability of underground fighters to move around inside the country.

Future guerrilla attacks against South Africa are certain to be accompanied by urban terrorism. Attempts will be made to assassinate policemen and to attack Europeans at random by setting off bombs in restaurants, supermarkets, movie theaters, and similar places. Sporadic attempts at sabotage, begun in the 1960s, may well be stepped up in order to weaken white resolve, disrupt industrial production, and interfere with the operation of essential services. This type of warfare, however, is subject to severe limitations, even if revolutionaries were able to solve the difficult technical problems involved in starting such a campaign under South African conditions. The civilian population, including the African people, are likely to be alienated by the disruption of essential services and indiscriminate killing. Hungry and homeless people, moreover, become more dependent on government relief, not less so.

A modern industrial economy can easily be hampered by sabotage, but it can only be put out of action by airpower applied on a gigantic scale. (Well-trained German saboteurs aided by widespread civilian resistance could not prevent French occupation of the Ruhr in 1923, and neither the German blitz nor "V" weapons—to give a more spectacular example—could knock out Great Britain in World War II, despite all prewar predictions.) Thus the ability of saboteurs to damage the South African economy is puny.

Some theoreticians believe that a well-planned campaign of urban terror might destroy the present mood of confidence among the whites. Even though physical damage might be kept within tolerable bounds, it is argued that European morale would disintegrate if enough bombs were set off in supermarkets and movie houses. Past experience in Kenya, wartime experience in occupied Europe, or present-day occurrences in Ulster, Lebanon, or Israel, however, suggest that terror pays only temporary dividends, and that ordinary men and women can adjust to perils with astonishing resilience.

Alternatively, urban guerrillas might concentrate on murdering police officers and their families. According to theoreticians of terrorism like Carlos Marighella, the police would thus be provoked into taking repressive measures that, in turn, would cause the police to be more hated by the people and would thereby accelerate a breakdown of police morale. Irish guerrillas adopted this strategy during the Anglo-Irish hostilities of 1919–1921, with the result that the Royal Irish Constabulary simply collapsed. The Irish precedent, however, cannot be easily reproduced in South Africa. The morale of the Irish police had already been weakened by a government policy of financial stringency, by government insistence on submitting all security work to the test of political expediency, and by the hostility to which the police had been exposed in the press, in Parliament, and in many courts and juries. The South African establishment is better organized, more cohesive, and more efficient than the former British "ascendancy" in Ireland. The tasks of breaking down police morale and establishing "no-go" areas in South African towns would be infinitely more difficult than they were then in Ireland.

In the future, guerrillas may well prove to be a serious nuisance to South Africans.[16] Partisans may be expected to increase small-scale attacks as well as to create a certain amount of urban terrorism, possibly supplemented by "external efforts" such as attacks on South African consulates and the overseas headquarters of South African firms. Guerrillas may also attempt to hijack South African planes or to sabotage South African ships. They will intensify their attacks in the future. One day South Africa may have to face convergent raids from Mozambique, Rhodesia, Botswana, and Namibia, with foreign military formations—Cuban, Nigerian, and such—stationed on the republic's doorstep. The effectiveness of guerrilla raids, however, is strictly limited, as the Israeli example has shown. South Africa probably has contingency plans for strikes against neighboring bases in the event of all-out war, or even the kind of war that gets into the headlines in the Middle East. South African resources are much greater than Israel's, and its geographical size is almost sixty times greater; hence South Africans can rely upon defense in depth in a manner unthinkable to the Israelis. Partisans, however well organized, can paralyze neither the economy, the armed forces, nor the state. Theoreticians of guerrilla warfare argue that South Africa cannot possibly wage an anti-insurgency campaign while at the same time maintaining a sophisticated industrial economy, given the relative paucity of the country's white population. This argument, however, ignores the experience of Rhodesia, which—contrary to the forecasts made by most of the real or assumed experts—managed for fourteen years to resist an international boycott and the assaults of partisans from abroad, strengthen its armed forces, and at the same time expand and diversify its economy, even though the proportion of whites to blacks in Rhodesia was much smaller (1 : 24) than it is in South Africa (1 : 5).

Given the present conditions, hopes for a violent overthrow of the South African system—either by a foreign invasion or by internal or external guerrilla assaults—belong in the realm of military fantasy.

5
South Africa in World Politics

One of the most intriguing features of international politics in the years following World War I has been the emergence of the pariah state. Pariah states (as we noted earlier) are countries that have been subjected to varying degrees of ostracism, ostensibly on humanitarian grounds. For a time, the Western powers attempted to place East Germany in this category, since it was an artificial creation whose government was sustained solely by the force of Soviet tanks. The German Democratic Republic has since acquired international legitimacy, and the label is now applied solely to pro-Western countries that for one reason or another have incurred special displeasure on the part of the Soviet bloc or Third World nations. Rhodesia and the Transkei have not received any international recognition, even though much more oppressive ministates like Albania, Burundi, or Equatorial Guinea have had no such difficulties. South Korea and Taiwan also have strong claims to be considered part of the family; their very existence has been widely challenged. Chile and Iran have become partial outcasts on account of their authoritarian governments. Israel has been spared full membership in the outcasts' club because of the influence of her superpower patron.

Of all these nations, South Africa has perhaps elicited the most dislike from the United Nations, the powers of the Warsaw Pact, and those Western liberals who always see the mote in the eye of their ally and never the beam in the eye of their enemy. Given the power of the liberal establishment in academia, the television networks, the prestige press, and the establishment churches, the notion of an entente with South Africa—a policy that was considered most advantageous to this country in World War II—has become unthinkable. The United Nations has declared an arms boycott against South

Africa, though not against such bloodthirsty African dictatorships as Uganda or Equatorial Guinea or the Central African Empire. The U.S. government stands committed to changing the existing system of government in the Republic of South Africa.

There is not, however, the slightest reason why the West should play the pariah-state game. South Africa is certainly not the most tyrannical country in the Third World—not to speak of the Second World. A political prisoner wise to the ways of the world would certainly prefer to be interned on Robben Island rather than in a camp run by the People's Republic of China, Uganda, or even the Soviet Union.[1] In more practical terms, South Africa occupies a major place in the world economy, and an equally important place in international strategy. Many Western commentators disagree with this assumption, and seek to play down South Africa's actual or potential importance to the West. They widely disparage the apparent Soviet menace to the Cape route, or the importance of Soviet and Cuban influence in Angola and, to a much lesser extent, in Mozambique. They argue that overseas bases are an anachromism in an age of nuclear-powered submarines; these vessels, after all, can cruise vast distances, far from their home ports, for extensive periods of time. This analysis, however, underestimates the importance of nonnuclear ships still in use, and of local air cover. It makes too little of limited confrontations, or of the political use of naval power to support friendly regimes in countries like Ethiopia, or of the intimidation of weaker states on the Indian Ocean littoral.

The future uses of Soviet naval power are many. For instance, the USSR—perhaps in concert with other nations and conceivably even with the backing of a liberal administration in the United States—might possibly obtain in the remote future a mandate from the UN to blockade South Africa. The feasibility of such a policy has already been discussed, together with its economic impact. Suffice it to say at this point that such action would be undertaken, ostensibly with other "progressive" powers, to crush apartheid. It would in fact destabilize the whole of Southern Africa and deny to the West the resources of South Africa at a time when it supplies vital strategic mineral resources to the noncommunist world.

Soviet policy shifts and fluctuates, but there is a clear general line based on the assumption that détente requires intensification of the international class struggle, not its lessening. The Communist Party of the Soviet Union and the communist parties of its allies all hold, moreover, that the socialist states must continue to strengthen their strategic superiority over the Western powers, that the military balance of power now favors the Warsaw Pact over NATO, and that the Warsaw Pact's power must be augmented. Soviet strategic doctrines are offensive in nature; they emphasize the ability of the Soviet Union to carry out sustained assaults by land, sea, and air. A friendly South

Africa, capable of holding its own in the military sense, is therefore of distinct value to the Western interests both in the strategic field and in the area of supplies.

The Soviet Union's aim is to deny South African resources to the NATO powers. The loss to the Western world of Southern Africa's minerals, port facilities, and similar resources, would be serious enough in itself; but were these riches to be added to the Soviet sphere, the USSR would obtain a staggering addition to its economic power.

By some quirk of nature, the Soviet Union and South Africa are major sources of several vital minerals. Together they produce more than 90 percent of the world's platinum, 60 percent of the world's gem diamonds, 40 percent of its industrial diamonds, about 80 percent of the world's gold, and sizable percentages of global supplies of asbestos, uranium, fluorspar, and other metals. Soviet control over the Cape route would also enable the Kremlin to pressure NATO and OPEC (Organization of Petroleum Exporting Countries) states by a Soviet threat to hamper or interrupt maritime traffic.[2]

A Soviet-backed blockade of South Africa, sanctioned by the UN and supported by the conscience vote in the United States on campuses, in churches, and by the media, no longer seemed unthinkable in 1978. Indeed, attacks against foreign investors in South Africa and Namibia could provide ideological legitimacy for UN-sanctioned naval intervention. Angolan and Mozambican ports would then be of inestimable value to blockading forces in much the same way that Freetown in Sierra Leone once served the British West African Squadron in its struggle against the slave trade. New bases in South Africa would serve gunboat diplomacy, which could be used to put pressure on incumbent governments; these bases would also be useful for gun running, for training revolutionary cadres, and for launching proxy forces —such as Cuban troops—in future adventures.

Angolan and Mozambican bases would benefit the Soviets from the standpoint of financial economy. The Soviet Admiralty would find it much cheaper to support a fleet of submarines from a nearby fixed base, furnished with ample stocks, machine shops, and dry-dock facilities, than from a distant home base. Access to an advanced base increases the "time-on-station," hence the effectiveness, of a submarine on patrol. Lower costs are an important feature in planning during peacetime, when Soviet strategists are well aware of the way in which military expenditures depress their sagging economy. In either a cold war or a hot war, overseas bases make possible faster turnaround and greater efficiency in rearming, restocking, and repairing ships; they can also serve as air bases to facilitate fleet reconnaissance and communications.

In the event of total war, facilities in Angola and Mozambique would increase the operational range of Soviet missile-carrying submarines. Soviet ships have mapped out the ocean floor and the currents of the Indian Ocean to learn where their submarines can hide from antisubmarine forces, and are doing similar work in the South Atlantic. They have learned, for example, that sonar-detection devices may be ineffective under certain hydrographic conditions in the Indian Ocean. Submarines concealed in these areas would form a potent strategic threat.

The new Soviet 4,900-mile missile aboard a Soviet submarine operating from Angola would introduce new strategic possibilities. A missile capable of striking the United States from a submarine operating in the Indian Ocean has not yet been developed, but it is technically feasible. U.S. planners would be better able to counteract these and similar threats if they had access to South African harbors and to the excellent naval base at Simonstown, as well as to the vast complex of South African airfields and industrial and repair facilities.

In summary, bases in South Africa would supply the United States with permanent facilities from which American ships and aircraft could operate. Ships and crews would not have to be shuttled from the United States or from Europe to the Indian Ocean, and from Atlantic to Indian Ocean ports, if South Africa's ample supply and repair facilities were made available. U.S. naval forces would save on fuel and resupply requirements, as well as on man-hours and ship-hours lost in transit. Crews could be changed periodically through the use of aircraft. The U.S. strategic position in the Indian Ocean and the South Atlantic would be strengthened. Surveillance and defense of the Cape route would be vastly facilitated. The United States could rely on an extensive industrial and military infrastructure and on substantial local forces.

The advantages of South African cooperation are now denied to the West because of internal and external policy. No black African government is willing or able to provide the kind of facilities that South Africa could furnish to the Western alliance in the South Atlantic and the Indian Ocean. The questions then remain: Will the cost of military self-denial exceed the price? And will South Africa succeed in averting the long-heralded revolution that would range black against white?

The case against Western cooperation with South Africa seems strong. It is said that, militarily, cooperation with a white regime in Africa is unnecessary. The Soviets do not need South Africa to interrupt Western oil supplies. In any case, the Soviet navy is not likely to interrupt the flow of oil around the Cape except in the event of a major war between the two superpowers. Such a conflict would certainly involve the use of nuclear weapons; it would be a clash of apocalyptic dimensions, terrifying beyond the imagination of man. An all-out American-Soviet war is unthinkable, and should therefore be excluded from the calculations of Western policy makers. It is true that the

Soviet Union may be increasing its relative strength in Africa, but does this really matter to the United States? Would an American failure to maintain a particular government in Zaïre, Nigeria, or South Africa really alter the global balance of power?

There are also economic arguments against American–South African cooperation. The entire African continent has always occupied a minor position in America's total trade and investment, as we will discuss later. Suffice it to say here that American investors have put more money into the United Kingdom alone than into the whole of Africa. The $1.24 billion of direct private American investment in Africa in 1973 represented 1.2 percent of private American investment overseas (yielding 1.0 percent of private earnings), and only 16 percent of all foreign investment in South Africa.[3] (By 1977, American investments were estimated, in book terms, at $1.6 billion dollars; their market and replacement value would, of course, be considerably higher.) U.S. trade with the entire African continent is likewise but a small fraction of American commerce with the European Economic Community (EEC). U.S.–South African trade, in turn, is only a fraction of America's total traffic with Africa. Nigeria is more important than South Africa as a supplier of raw materials (especially oil), and as a consumer of American merchandise (see table 10).

Protesters claim that the Americans would be foolish to alienate black Africa and progressives both at home and abroad—not to speak of American blacks—for the sake of sustaining a tyrannical white regime on the southern tip of Africa. In any case, they claim, white rule in Africa is doomed. Sooner or later, Washington will have to deal with a black revolutionary government in Pretoria. Even if such a government were anti-American, there would be no reason for a militantly left-wing successor government to cease trading with the United States: the Marxist-Leninist government now installed in Angola is only too anxious to deal with Gulf Oil, an American-controlled oil concern that operates in the Cabinda enclave.

American support for South Africa, this argument concludes, would be

TABLE 10

U.S. COMMERCE, 1974
(in million dollars)

Direction	African Continent	South Africa	Nigeria	EEC
Imports to	2,180	377	652	21,700
Exports from	1,235	746	161	14,250

SOURCE: U.S. Department of Commerce, Bureau of the Census, *Statistical Abstracts of the United States* (July 1975), table 8.

economically ill advised, militarily unsound, and morally perverse. The United States should therefore frame a new African policy—one that would look upon the needs of the continent as a whole and avoid alienating the Third World for the sake of pleasing a handful of white reactionaries outside and within the borders of South Africa.

We remain unconvinced by these arguments. The development of nuclear weapons has not made conventional war obsolete; there have been numerous large-scale conventional conflicts since the end of World War II. The fates of South Korea, Israel, and South Vietnam have so far been decided by great battles of a kind that would have been intelligible to the strategists of the Second World War. Africa continues to be a major strategic asset, a fact well known to Soviet military leadership. Critics of cooperation between the United States and South Africa argue that the political costs of such an association would outweigh the strategic advantages, yet no independent African government can present the West with equivalent resources. Even though American trade and investment in South Africa are not great in terms of American enterprise in the world at large, South Africa plays an important part in the economic well-being of the EEC.

U.S. policy makers will have to eschew the notion of formulating an all-Africa diplomatic policy. The many African countries are disparate in size and importance, none of them are nation-states in the Western sense. All of them are multiethnic communities, and all of them—including South Africa—are colonial creations that owe their very existence to imperial conquest. Their roots in the past are shallow. Few African nationalists have been able or even willing to restore the kingdoms or principalities of precolonial Africa. Liberal democracy based on the principle of "one man, one vote" works best in developed nations that have a strong sense of historical continuity and are reasonably homogeneous, or believe themselves to be reasonably homogeneous, in ethnic composition. (Switzerland, one of the very few exceptions, solves its national problems by providing its various ethnic groups with a great array of "homelands" in the form of cantons that enjoy a wide measure of internal autonomy.) The "one man, one vote" principle is hard to apply successfully in multiethnic or religiously divided countries like Cyprus or Lebanon or Malaya, where men vote according to their ethnic or religious affinity, where all political questions turn out to be ethnic questions, and where even socialism is apt to become ethnic socialism. Liberal democracy met with similar obstacles when it was applied to the multiethnic states that emerged from the breakup of the Ottoman and the Austro-Hungarian monarchies, and it has been no more successful in the multiethnic states that developed out of the Western empires in Africa. (Botswana, a rare exception, is one of the few multiparty states left in Africa. Its parliamentary institutions work like Western ones because the Tswana are a reasonably homogeneous people, unlike the Kenyans, the Zambians, or the Zaïrians, who are divided into competing ethnic groups and who owe their statehood solely to the now-departed imperial *pax*.)

The problems of these various states differ widely. No single political formula will meet all their needs, and American policy makers should not seek to apply such a formula. In any case, only a few African nations are of major importance to the United States: Zaïre, Nigeria, and South Africa. Policies for these states should not be constructed on an all-African basis; the United States should treat these countries as independent powers, just as it deals with individual European countries. South Africa is likely to remain the major power of sub-Saharan Africa. As we have tried to demonstrate, the South African establishment is not likely to be overthrown for a long time to come, if at all. The opposition is divided. The army and the administration are neither inefficient, corrupt, nor subject to revolutionary infiltration—unlike, say, the former governmental apparatus of South Vietnam. The country's military expenditures, though impressive by African standards, do not constitute an insupportable burden. South Africa is not on the point of breakdown. Despite predictions of a racial bloodbath, the whites have managed the country with infinitely less violence than has occurred in independent African countries such as Nigeria, the Sudan, Zaïre, Burundi, Uganda, or Angola.

The point bears repeating that South Africa remains a progressive society in economic terms. South Africa's dynamic quality sharply distinguishes it from so many newly independent African countries—Marxist and non-Marxist alike—that have permitted their economies to run down. In the late 1950s and the early 1960s, the bulk of Western academicians and policy makers concerned with Africa assumed, as a matter of faith, that independence would usher in a new era of "nation building," "mobilization," economic growth, and peaceful development. Some African states, Kenya and the Ivory Coast, for example, have indeed done well since the departure of their former imperial masters. Many other countries, however, have had to pay a heavy price for liberation (for instance, Angola, Mozambique, Zaïre, and Equatorial Guinea). In many cases independence has entailed the rise of a new parasitic class of party functionaries, bureaucrats, and ideologues whose ill-considered interference has brought about economic decline. Peasants are reluctant to grow cash crops if they can only sell them at prices pegged below market value. Investors hesitate to risk their savings if they are subject to sudden expropriation, or to bribes and taxation of a confiscatory kind. The exodus of former "colonialists" from Zaïre, Angola, and Mozambique has deprived these countries of technicians, specialists, and entrepreneurs whose skills are now badly missed. Above all, countries as diverse in their political philosophies as Zaïre and Mozambique now have to cope with widespread lawlessness, banditry, and loss of worker morale. The breakdown of law and order is apt to have consequences that are poorly understood by academicians working in the safety of Western university campuses or habituated to doing field work in the security of the bygone imperial era.. The very disparity in the documentation available for, say, Zaïre, on the one hand, and South Africa, on the other, has indeed created distortions. Academicians interested in South Africa are able to draw on a great wealth of government reports, sociological surveys, and official inquiries that reveal the country's ills. Journalists can travel about South Africa in relative security. Corresponding material does not exist in anything like comparable quantities for Angola and Zaïre. Anthropologists and journalists do not readily take trips into the outlying parts of Zaïre or, for that matter, into Burundi or Equatorial Guinea. The very availability of information concerning South Africa thus creates informational distortions.

South Africans are rightly concerned, however, at the price of black liberation—a price that foreign critics rarely consider and are never themselves obliged to pay. Americans should therefore take another look at the vexed question of whether they should support present U.S. policies that seek speedy, and indeed revolutionary, changes in Southern Africa. An alternative to potential disaster must be found. In our view it makes greater political sense to support the moderates than to favor the radicals in South Africa, and indeed, in Rhodesia and Namibia.

South Africa seems increasingly to be torn by internal conflict, but this is a situation the United States and the West should seek to prevent; a racial war in the country must be avoided. Nevertheless, consensus cannot be achieved in South Africa's multiracial, multiethnic society at this time. Ethnic complexities are further complicated by struggles between classes that are divided along color lines. Whites, who own most of the land and control most of the economy, fear that any political surrender will lead to the loss of their economic control and their culture. They cannot agree among themselves, much less with any other social faction. Ethnic polarization is increasing. Antiwhite feelings are strong and have recently led to a coalition between the Coloured Labour Party, the Indian Reform Party and the Zulu Inkatha movement designed to draw up a new constitution for a "non-racist" society. For a consensus to be reached, individuals in the various racial, economic, and political groups would have to stand apart from those groups on important issues in order to act for the benefit of the larger unit of South Africa. It is hard to imagine Afrikaners thinking of themselves as citizens of a nation rather than as members of their ethnic group, but if they fail to transcend these narrower loyalties, South Africa's future may be bleak. Because conflict will not resolve the country's problems and consensus may be impossible to achieve, a third way should be tried—a consociational system.

Consociation implies continued social and ethnic diversity, based on a policy of pragmatism and tempered by cooperation between the elites in each social group. These elites could act as brokers to limit conflict and to reach accommodation and a balance of power between their conflicting interests. The consociational state would require the exercise of a joint veto and local autonomy for each group, and proportional representation. Such a solution would, however, face great difficulties. The whites would hold disproportionate influence since they command so much of the country's property and so much of its managerial and technical skills. Blacks could thus argue that even this moderate solution would be merely white supremacy in disguise. Calls for a class or race war would be hard to ignore.

Can a peaceful South Africa be created in the future? It can, but it will be a difficult task. A successful regime will have to recognize the diversity of South Africa's ethnic, political, and economic groups, and will have to mediate between them. The striking differences in status and material wealth between blacks, browns, and whites will gradually have to be reduced. Political power cannot be restricted to whites and to traditional tribal rulers; leadership roles must be shared among all group elites. South Africa will have to accept a federal system, but not one based only on the homelands (Bantustans) concept. All racially discriminatory legislation and practices will have to be ended. Some progress has already been made toward the last goal; for example, segregation has ended in some hotels, bars, and restaurants. Legislation such as the Group Areas Act and the Mixed Marriages and Immorality Acts, however, must also be repealed. In short, apartheid will have to be dismantled. Strong efforts need to be made to build a South African consciousness and to stress nationalism based on equality before the law and on human rights.

This complicated, delicate process of accommodation, power sharing, and leveling can only succeed if all groups agree to cooperate. This will not be easy in a multiracial, ethnically diverse society—a society that has long been dominated by whites and is under attack by the SACP, the ANC, and the PAC, as well as by radical states and the UN. Nevertheless, there are some grounds for hope.

Reform in South Africa will come from within. It will derive from the ruling Nationalist party rather than from a divided opposition. The Nationalist party is not a monolithic bloc, run, like a communist party, on the rigid principles of "democratic centralism." The party is being transformed by those social and economic forces that shape and reshape South African society as a whole. Half a century ago the Afrikaners were mainly rural people. The average Nationalist voter was an indigent farmer, a white workman often without a job, an employee, a teacher, or a rural clergyman. In certain respects, the Nationalist party resembled a pre–World War II peasant party in Eastern Europe—anti-capitalist, anti-urban, ethnocentric, and anti-semitic. In the meantime, the Afrikaners have moved into the towns; they have risen in the social sphere; the "poor white," fearful of African competition and Negrophobe in outlook, has largely disappeared. The Nationalist party today is a coalition that contains bankers, factory owners, and professional men, as well as white workers and farmers. The conservative wing remains strong in the caucus, the cultural organizations, the civil service and the police; it derives support from white workers, employees, and from small farmers. But there is now a substantial reformist group made up of businessmen, professional people, technicians and specialists both in the public and private sector, clergymen, and also members of the defense establishment anxious to strengthen the country's industrial power and determined to create a wider social consensus. The Nationalist party no longer speaks of combating the Jews or repatriating the Indians. Whatever the party's failings, it has done more in the field of African slum clearance, the expansion of social services for Africans, Indians, and Coloureds, and the economic development of the rural African areas than all its supposedly more liberal predecessors. Among young Afrikaners engaged in rural development schemes there is a genuine spirit of idealism and a degree of technical competence that puts the Peace Corps to shame. These social changes are reflected in Afrikaner politics.

In the recent election the extreme right-wing (HNP) party failed to win a single seat. Opinion polls in South Africa in December 1977 showed that 70 percent of Nationalist supporters are ready for significant changes in official race policies. Job-reservation categories have been abolished; the minister of justice said he is prepared to revise the detention laws, and the prime minister has been holding discussions with Indians and Coloured leaders on constitutional proposals. Black trade unions will be recognized. Among the most significant changes for the better were Vorster's appointments to his new cabinet. Dr. C. P. Mulder, a pragmatist and a moderate, was appointed to a key post—that of handling the government's relations with the nation's nineteen million Africans. Another moderate, W. A. Cruywagen, was put in charge of African education. F. W. De Klerk, who is also a pragmatist and a moderate, was added to the cabinet, and the most powerful right-wing politician of the cabinet, Andries Treurnicht, was ignored—he remains a deputy minister with little power.

6

The United States and South Africa

How, then, should Americans react to the South African situation? Clergy-men call for sanctions. Students demand "divestment." Militants agitate for revolution. We see the problem in a very different light. We are struck by the curious American ethnocentricity that prevails on so many college campuses. There is a form of inverted American chauvinism in which all the world's evils are interpreted in terms of the real or supposed wrongs committed by American investors and American spies. According to this interpretation, South Africa—or, for that matter, Iran, Chile, or Greece—would speedily become happy and contented democracies if only the Elders of Wall Street and the CIA were to cease their plotting. American ethnocentricity has other forms. It is characterized, for instance, by the assumption that a system of franchise and of political organization that functions well in this country would be equally successful in a multiethnic and multiracial country like South Africa.

White South Africans, however, are convinced that a "one man, one vote" system would imply ethnic suicide for them, that a powerless white minority would be treated by the ruling blacks no better than the Indians were treated in Uganda, and that black rule would entail civil war and economic collapse. The whites may be wrong in their assumptions, but given the experiences of postcolonial Zanzibar (where the Arab minority was destroyed), Burundi (where the Hutu were cruelly persecuted), Northern Nigeria (where the Ibo were robbed or massacred), or Algeria, Angola, and Mozambique (where the European population was compelled to emigrate), white fears are not unreasonable and should be treated with respect rather than with the con-tempt they receive from so many American intellectuals.

In our view, American interests, political and humanitarian, would best be served by the kind of "convergence" diplomacy so many liberals advocate with regard to the Soviet Union. We should quietly press for improvements in return for economic favors. We should extend rather than diminish academic, cultural, athletic, diplomatic, and economic contacts with South Africa. We should be conciliatory in tone and firm in intention. The gradual ending of apartheid, more education and job opportunities for blacks and Coloureds, more self-government for urban blacks, and more democracy in the homelands: these are attainable goals. Quiet diplomacy will achieve more than harangues in the UN. The Carter-Mondale-Young approach suffers from many disadvantages. It has the besetting sin of many American policies abroad—an apparent lack of clear purpose. (Foreign policy makers complain privately that they cannot always discern exactly what Americans want.) Yet the U.S. approach has been sufficiently menacing to white South Africans to harden their resolve at the same time that it is encouraging blacks in unrealistic expectations, thus weakening the middle ground of discussion and compromise. Public pressure on the Soviet Union has not won many concessions from Brezhnev; is it likely to make Vorster more conciliatory?

The difficulties in applying morality to diplomacy are many. Few governments outside of Western Europe and North America are democratic. Few governments are moral or just, or rule for the benefit of their people. If we do not deal with Chile, we can hardly deal with any communist regime. If we stop talking to South Africans because of their racial policies then we have to stop talking to half the nations of the world who oppress their minorities, their political opposition movements, their religious bodies, or persons who own property. A self-imposed suspension of moral judgments should regulate the relations between states.

Similarly, it is not reasonable to utilize economic boycotts as a means of conducting international relations. As the Israeli ambassador to the United States, Mr. Chaim Herzog, said during the debate on the resolution to condemn Israel for trading with South Africa:

> If preservation of human rights were to be the criterion for international trade, the world would be in a sorry state economically for there would be little trade indeed.

We should press for minor reforms in the hope that piecemeal changes will have a multiplying effect. We should use the carrot instead of the stick— that is, try to accelerate change through increased, not lessened, foreign investment in South Africa. By pouring in vast sums of money, we could cause the economy to expand so rapidly that there would be more funds for government services and a greater need for skilled workers than the white population could fill. White trade unions would allow blacks to enter the skilled trades, for example, if there were more jobs than the whites could handle. This has happened informally in South Africa in recent years; blacks now dominate industries that a few years ago excluded them—for example, the garment industry, the railroads, the post office, the mining and building industries, and the motor-repair business.

The Carter administration has taken a very different line because it is highly moralistic and mistakes South Africa for Georgia. South Africa's problems are not those of the American black minority seeking civil rights in the 1960s. In South Africa the blacks are the majority, and many are still basically tribal peoples. American blacks were and are a fully Americanized minority who speak English. Millions of blacks in South Africa live half in the tribal world and half in the modern world; they are divided into eleven major ethnic groups or nations, and English or Afrikaans is their second or third language. American policy makers are mistaken, therefore, in thinking that South Africa can be restructured by a new breed of twentieth-century abolitionists.

The Carter administration has swung back to the policy of petty harrassment followed during the Kennedy and Johnson eras. It has given unequivocal support to majority rule in South Africa—though not in any other Second or Third World nation. The Transkei has been refused recognition; there has been a tightened arms embargo on South Africa; U.S. corporations doing business in South Africa are being pressured, the president and Congress criticize South Africa and join UN boycotts. Yet this policy of harrassment has failed in the past. It will fail in the future, with a resultant hardening of white rule over blacks, Indians, and Coloureds. Vorster's regime arrested six hundred people during the week after the UN imposed a tougher boycott on arms for South Africa.

American investments in South Africa occupy too small a place (16 percent of the total foreign holdings) to be a major bargaining counter; South Africa today can generate the bulk of its own capital and even export it. Past restrictions on American arms sales have not only deprived the United States of a market, but have forced South Africa to develop a major arms industry of its own—in cooperation with the French. An American trade embargo on South Africa is not likely to succeed. The balance of trade is in favor of the United States rather than against it; what the United States supplies, moreover, can readily be obtained from other sources, whereas it needs South Africa's minerals. Formal trade embargoes have been violated by many African states who do a $1.5 billion business with South Africa each year. Embargoes are no more likely to succeed than were American attempts to coerce Cuba, or than the Stalinist attempts to subjugate Yugoslavia by economic means.

George W. Ball put his finger on what is wrong with Carter's policy.

"Diplomacy, like politics, is the art of the possible, and if we use our leverage toward an unachievable end, we will create a mess."[1] A peaceful but imperfect solution for South Africa is preferable to a perfect solution achieved by violent means. The United States is not likely to give military support to blacks in their effort to overthrow the whites; yet by our diplomacy we have alienated the whites, and we will alienate the blacks when we fail to support their war of liberation against Pretoria. Nothing short of armed intervention by a major power in support of African nationalists can achieve the formula of "one man, one vote," so why insist on it? Who wants a bloody war in South Africa? Why, after our Vietnam experience, have we adopted a moral interventionist stance?

Is the disruption of South Africa truly in the American interest? South Africa presently controls the Cape route, a major consideration, as we have shown, at a time when Soviet naval power has become influential in the western part of the Indian Ocean, and it is the only African country capable during wartime of supplying its allies in the western part of the Indian Ocean with a vast industrial infrastructure. It plays a major role in the global economy as the world's greatest producer of gold, and as a major exporter of uranium, diamonds, chrome, manganese, and other minerals. The West would be ill served if we should help to turn South Africa into yet another Angola—from which the whites fled or were expelled and where a civil war continues to rage—at a time when Soviet strategists are rightly convinced that the military balance of power, once so unfavorable to them, has swung their way. South Africa's policy may offend the governments of countries like Guinea and Rwanda, which, between them, wield two paper votes at the UN; but the real power—as opposed to the voting power—of all African countries is small, and the Western nations cannot afford to buy their capricious favor by concessions that would further weaken the West itself.

Moreover, as we have pointed out before, the United States has a legitimate interest in a secure passage around the Cape of Good Hope and in access to the mineral wealth of Southern Africa for itself and its allies. American reliance on imported minerals is on the increase. It is, of course, perfectly true that up to now communist and procommunist powers have made no attempt to halt the supply of strategic raw materials to the United States in pursuance of political objectives. In the long run, however, the danger for America of a growing dependence on raw materials that are controlled by hostile powers is very real—given the communists' assumption that trade, like cultural contacts and conventional diplomacy, is a legitimate weapon in "the intensification of the international class struggle" against the so-called "forces of imperialism."

In our opinion, the United States should take a "correct" and careful stance toward South Africa; our policy should overtly be based on our national interests and strategic requirements. The administration has an obligation to point out to the American public what our interests are, and how they should be safeguarded. We would be unwise to exaggerate the current strategic situation and South Africa's strategic importance in order to achieve a policy of rapprochement with that country for military reasons. Advocacy of close U.S. defense contacts with South Africa is politically unrealistic at this time and would both please our foes abroad and arouse bitter dissension at home. In the future, the United States should reconsider its policies in accordance with changing strategic needs.

The Carter administration believes that any form of cooperation with South Africa must be rejected because of the need to safeguard American relations with the independent black states of Africa, and indeed with all the nations of the Third World. It makes no sense, this argument states, to endanger, say, our growing trade with Nigeria, a country important for its oil, for the sake of propping up an endangered white regime in South Africa. The argument has some merit. The trade of black Africa as a whole is more valuable to the leading Western powers than their commerce with South Africa alone. The point is illustrated again by table 11.

The Western powers, however, cannot reasonably be expected to align their trade to correspond with the political preferences of other powers. The United States successfully insists on having commercial intercourse alike with Israel and the Arab powers, China and the Soviet Union, Algeria and Morocco, and so forth. African states likewise trade according to their notions of legitimate self-interest. Zambia imports mining machinery from South Africa not because the Zambians admire Pretoria's racial policies, but because the Zambian mining economy depends on South African supplies.

TABLE 11

TRADE WITH AFRICA, SOUTH AFRICA, AND NIGERIA, 1975
(in million dollars)

	All Africa (except South Africa)	South Africa	Nigeria
United States:			
Imports from	8,000	587	3,525
Exports to	2,904	1,193	536
United Kingdom:			
Imports from	2,725	1,494	1,130
Exports to	2,952	1,229	1,389
Japan:			
Imports from	1,663	880	520
Exports to	1,806	873	585

SOURCE: Henry Bienen, "United States Foreign Policy in Changing Africa," unpublished paper kindly made available to the writers by the author.

Mozambique—as we stated before—sends labor migrants to the Witwatersrand not because FRELIMO approves of South Africa's political attitudes, but because Mozambique needs South African technical skills and South African gold. The Soviet bloc countries themselves do not hesitate to trade with South Africa in a covert manner (for instance through Dutch and Yugoslav entrepôts); so do many other African nations. Indeed a whole new international service industry has grown up, an industry that specializes in falsifying bills of lading, altering labels, and publishing misleading statistics; it is this industry that enables revolutionary or quasi-revolutionary regimes to reconcile militant rhetoric with economic facts.

American diplomacy would, in fact, be well advised to insist, at international gatherings, on the legitimacy of the American national interest. There is little merit in interpreting our relations with the Soviet Union as a kind of international beauty competition, in which the Third World nations act as judges. In the long run, even the neutral powers depend for their continued existence as sovereign states on America's ability to hold the line against the growing power of the Soviet Union. Soviet military theoreticians are convinced that the balance of power is swinging against the West and toward the Soviet bloc. Chinese communists agree, and call upon NATO to strengthen its defenses. The West would do well to heed their warning.

In terms of morality, South Africa, for all its restrictions, is a great deal freer than Cuba, or the Soviet Union, or Angola, or Mozambique, not to mention scores of noncommunist African countries such as the bloodstained tyrannies that govern Burundi, Equatorial Guinea, or the Central African Empire. As we stated before, it is surely inconsistent to argue that the Soviet system should be rendered more amenable to Western values by a policy of trade or détente, but that such a policy should not apply to South Africa. Equally inconsistent is another argument we have frequently heard from liberals and leftists—that through trade and cultural relations we can bring about a convergence of our system and the Soviet one, but that the same policy should not be used toward South Africa.

The historical facts provide a starkly different picture. There is little evidence that convergence is occurring between the Soviet system and ours. There is some evidence, however, that South Africa is changing—offering more rights and better conditions to its people. The Coloureds and Indians are being offered their own parliaments; petty apartheid is being dismantled. South African ethnic policies deserve criticism, but in comparison with the ethnic mass expulsions that have taken place in wartime USSR or in postwar Eastern Europe, or with the troubles that have recently beset multiethnic countries like Lebanon, Iraq, or Cyprus, the actions of the South Africans have not been so bad, even if we include the recent rounds of detentions, arrests, and bannings. Part of South Africa's problem is that most acts of aggression are reported fully there, whereas this is not the case in African dictatorships or in communist countries. Where in the communist world would the death of a political prisoner have led the state to make public its autopsy report and to hold a public hearing to question the secret police? Yet this was done in South Africa after the death of Steve Biko. South Africa has yet to engage in mass liquidations, either punitive or prophylactic. It is a more liberal country than the majority of those that fill the UN. It has fewer political prisoners, for example, than Cuba.

White South Africans are far from perfect; they deny basic human rights to blacks, Indians and Coloured. Nevertheless, they are no worse than many other regimes around the world.

Ironically, while critics decry the oppressed conditions of blacks in South Africa and ignore oppression elsewhere, the facts reveal that South African blacks are the best educated and most urbanized, and enjoy some of the best living conditions of any people on the entire continent of Africa—and these facts are admitted even by Marxist critics of the regime. Still, blacks in South Africa are politically discontented; they have no vote or say in running the government. They also resent the fact that they have significantly lower incomes than their white rulers. Conditions clearly must change in South Africa. We are all agreed on the end to be achieved: a just society in South Africa. We may, however, disagree on the best means to achieve this end.

There is no better hope for South Africa and for the world at large than the ascendancy of the moderates. Wherever radicals have come to power in recent years, bloodshed, expulsion, forced-labor camps, confiscation, and reeducation programs have resulted. The record of the radicals in Angola and Mozambique has been disastrous; in Ethiopia it has been barbaric, and elsewhere it has been inept, even if more humane.

The people of South Africa would probably be willing to cooperate if they felt that they were participating in the governing process through their representatives. As long as blacks can see that they are moving toward the ideals of justice, dignity, equality and freedom, they will work with the system and will not listen to the call to arms.

In our opinion, economic and social apartheid should be progressively dismantled. The Group Areas Act and the Mixed Marriages and Immorality Acts should be abrogated. Job reservations and other restrictions on blacks, Indian and Coloured businessmen should be abolished. There should be more education and greater opportunities for blacks and Coloureds. Urban blacks should be given more self-government, and political power should be shared in some measure by the whites with all the peoples of South Africa. The police need to be reformed. The government has to stop suppressing moderate opposition leaders and talk to them. The inane South African censorship system must also be changed.

Our approach rests on the assumption that South Africa can liberalize herself from within—that reforms are more likely to come from the ruling party than from an ineffective opposition or an international coalition. The United States should promote trade, economic cooperation, and cultural exchanges with South Africa of the kind we have adopted in our dealings with the Soviet Union. In the military and strategic sphere, we should deal with South Africa from the standpoint of a well-considered realpolitik.

The policy we have outlined will have real and continuing costs both domestically and in foreign relations. We recognize that these costs may be heavy, but we believe they are to be preferred to encouraging unrealistic expectations in Southern Africa or to following President Carter's present policies.

There is reason to hope. However much whites and blacks quarrel, they are at any rate beginning to struggle for the same things—the fruits of modern industrial civilization. An expanding economy is forcing both whites and blacks to cooperate on functional lines; the quest for improved living standards in which both groups participate forms the cement that holds the plural society together. It is the task of political leaders of all persuasions to strengthen these bonds, for the alternative is not some progressive utopia but a vicious struggle for power. Such battles have broken out in Namibia, Rhodesia, and South Africa; blacks may win in some regions and whites in others—there is nothing inevitable about a universal African victory. Whatever the outcome, however, the ultimate result can only be disaster; welfare, liberty, and the rights of man would disappear from the face of Southern Africa if the issues are decided by a racial war.

Notes

Preface

1. For the political alignment within the federal bureaucracy on Southern African questions, see, for instance, Anthony Lake, *The "Tar Baby" Option: American Policy Towards Southern Rhodesia* (New York: Columbia University Press, 1976).

Chapter 1: South Africa: A Pariah State?

No notes accompany this chapter.

Chapter 2: South Africa: Strategic and Economic Potential

1. In 1977 the Soviet strategic nuclear-submarine forces consisted of 78 submarines with 845 missiles; the U.S. strategic submarine forces consisted of 41 submarines with 656 missiles.

2. J. William Middendorf, "American Maritime Strategy and Soviet Naval Expansion," *Strategic Review*, Winter 1976, pp. 16–25.

3. Cited in David Rees, "Soviet Strategic Penetration in Africa," *Conflict Studies* 77 (November 1976): 4.

4. Alvin Cottrell, "Strategic Routes, Key Passages and Choke Points in and around Southern Africa: Threats Posed to Them by Hostile Local or External Forces," in Roger Pearson, ed., *Sino-Soviet Intervention in Africa* (Washington, D.C.: Council on American Affairs, 1977), pp. 46–47.

5. Robert Moss, "Fellow-Traveling in Mozambique," *National Review* 23 (December 1977).

6. Peter Vanneman and Martin James, "The Soviet Intervention in Angola: Intentions and Implications," *Strategic Review*, Summer 1976, pp. 92–103.

7. See William H. Lewis, "How a Defense Planner Looks at Africa," in Helen Kitchen, ed., *Africa: From Mystery to Maze*, vol. 12 of *Critical Choices for*

America (Lexington, Mass.: D. C. Heath and Co., 1976), pp. 277–309; by way of contrast, see Wolfgang Reith, "Die Bedeutung Südafrikas für die Verteidigung der westlichen Welt," *Europäische Wehrkunde* 26 (June 1977): 275–80.

Chapter 3: The Defensive Infrastructure

1. See South Africa, *White Paper on Defence, 1977* (Pretoria, 1977), p. 9. For Soviet military doctrines, see, for instance, Philip A. Karber, "Die taktische Revolution in der sowjetischen Militärdoktrin," *Europäische Wehrkunde* 26 (June 1977): 265–74. For Soviet strategic concepts, see, for instance, Richard Pipes, "Why the Soviet Union Thinks It Could Fight and Win a Nuclear War," *Commentary* 64, no. 1 (July 1977): 21–34.

2. In 1977 the South African government publicly promised that South Africa would use nuclear energy for peaceful purposes only, and would abstain from testing nuclear bombs. The South African minister of finance, Owen P. F. Harwood, on the other hand, indicated that his country would exert the right to use its nuclear potential in any manner it thought fit.

3. South Africa maintains virtually complete secrecy on its trade and consumption of oil. According to the Economist Intelligence Unit, *Interdependence in Southern Africa: Trade and Transport Links in South, Central and East Africa,* July 1976, p. 17, South Africa relies on oil for less than 25 percent of its energy requirements. This is expected to decrease to 20 percent by 1980. Of the existing energy requirements, 5 percent is supposedly produced by the oil-from-coal plant. The main suppliers were Iran, Saudi Arabia, Iraq, Qatar, and Abu Dhabi, in that order. The oil embargo adopted by the General Assembly of the UN in 1962 has had no serious effect on the country. Jonathan Baker, "Oil and African Development," *Journal of Modern African Studies* 15, no. 2, (1977): 175–212, provides detailed information regarding the oil potential of South Africa and of the continent as a whole, as well as South Africa's ability to withstand an oil boycott.

4. Estimated expenditures for the year 1977–1978 will be 1,711.7 million rands; this is 19.1 percent of all state expenditures and 5.1 percent of the GNP, compared with 5.3 percent of East Germany's expenditures, 5.4 percent of United States', 7.9 percent of Nigeria's, and 12 percent of the USSR's. Increases were as follows (in million rands):

	1975–1976	1976–1977	1977–1978
Total expenditures	1,043.5	1,407.6	1,711.7
Estimated percentage of state expenditures	15.0	17.0	19.0
Estimated percentage of GNP	4.1	4.9	5.1

SOURCE: *White Paper on Defence* (Pretoria, 1977), pp. 12, 14.

5. For weapons sold to South Africa from abroad, see the Stockholm Institute of Peace Research. For a list of major South African armament firms, shipbuilding firms and aerospace systems, as well as weapons and organization, see *Defense and Foreign Affairs Handbook, 1976–1977* (San Francisco: Copley Associates, 1977), pp. 413–15.

6. "Arms Embargo Comes Too Late to Affect South Africa," The *Washington Post*, 28 October 1977.

7. In 1977, 7 percent of the full-time men were members of the Permanent Force, 6.6 percent belonged to the National Service, and 3.1 percent were civilians. Of the part-time men, 54.9 percent were Citizen Force members and 28.3 percent were commandos, for a total of 83.2 percent.

8. According to the Johannesburg *Star*, 28 December 1974 (cited by Jordan K. Ngubane before the U. S. Congress, Senate Subcommittee on Africa, 94th Cong., 1st sess., June 1975, p. 417), in 1974 85 percent of the Permanent Force staff spoke Afrikaans and 15 percent spoke English. Among the generals and admirals, the proportions were 70 percent and 30 percent, respectively; in the air force 75 percent spoke Afrikaans and 25 percent spoke English; the navy contained equal numbers of Afrikaans speakers and English speakers.

9. Cynthia M. Enloe, "Ethnic Factors in the Evolution of the South African Military," *Issue* 5, no. 4 (Winter 1975): 21–28.

10. See Albie Sachs "The Machinery of White Domination in South Africa," in Leonard Thompson and Jeffrey Butler, eds., *Change in Contemporary South Africa* (Berkeley: University of California Press, 1975), pp. 223–49, for figures. For the Lumpa Church, see Andrew Roberts, *A History of Zambia* (London: Heinemann, 1976).

Chapter 4: South Africa: A Revolutionary Situation?

1. In August 1977 General Ignatius Acheampong promised increased training facilities in Ghana to SWAPO. Brigadier Shehu Musa Yar Adua, the Nigerian chief of staff, promised additional backing to the Southern African liberation movements in the form of financial, moral, and diplomatic support, as well as in military training. He also promised that the Nigerian army would intervene if any independent African state were to be attacked by a Southern African regime. He added that much as the Nigerian armed forces would like to fight alongside the liberation forces, the latter had not requested any such help. *FBIS-SSA* 77-148 (2 August 1977), p. D1.

2. According to recent estimates, by 1978 these comprised 20,000–22,000 Cubans. The Angolan army proper was estimated at about 32,000 men.

3. According to a study completed by the British Association of Industries in 1977, a boycott of South Africa would increase British unemployment by seventy thousand, as one of her most prosperous overseas markets (£600 million a year) would have to be sacrificed. South Africa would be most seriously affected in terms of fuel consumption, but even so, it is not as vulnerable as many observers think. South Africa does not run on oil. Of the country's energy needs, only one quarter is based on oil; the remaining three quarters are based on coal.

4. Rhodesia thus diversified her economic production in two world wars, when supplies from Great Britain became scanty. In a little-known ersatz industries venture, German East Africa created a whole range of small-scale substitute manufactures during World War I when the infant colony was totally cut off from

the *Reich* and yet managed to carry on with the help of local resources for about two years.

5. According to social-distance tests carried out by M. L. Edelstein, a South African sociologist, educated Coloureds identify more readily with English-speaking South African whites than with Afrikaners, Jews, or Africans. Indians likewise identify more with English-speaking white South Africans than with Coloureds, city Africans, Jews, Afrikaners, or tribal Africans, in that order. Africans (that is, African matriculants from Soweto) feel about as close to English-speaking South African whites as to Coloureds—followed by Jews, Afrikaners, and Indians. Of course, tests of this kind have only limited value. Attitudes change, as respondents change their minds. Even in Angola, however, where the class struggle is supposed to have transcended ethnic considerations, the MPLA was forced to conduct a purge against black nationalists, leaving the balance of power with the mestiço (mixed blood) group within the ruling party. (See Melville Leonard Edelstein, *What do Young Africans Think?* [Johannesburg: Labour and Community Consultants, 1974].)

6. Anthony Sampson, *The Treason Cage: The Opposition Trial in South Africa* (London: Heinemann, 1958), includes an appendix listing the social background of 156 leaders accused in the treason trial that lasted from 1956 to 1961. Full statistical accuracy is not possible on the basis of the information given, but certain features clearly emerge. The oppositional leadership came almost entirely from the towns; only three of the men in the dock made their living by farming. The largest professional group was made up of clerks, who numbered at least 35 out of the original 156, and probably more. There was a large group of professionals—about 36 persons—composed almost entirely of physicians, clergymen, teachers, and journalists. Leadership in modern industry was represented by a solitary industrial chemist. Altogether, the white-collar occupations accounted for at least 93 out of the original 156, including the great majority of the leaders. The working-class element may have included about 28 persons, 9 of whom appear to have been unskilled and 14 factory workers or truck drivers; only 5 people would be ranked as highly skilled, and they were employed mainly in jobs on the industrial periphery, such as cabinetmaking, dressmaking, and photography. The "strategic" industries were not significantly represented. There were also some 29 people variously described as "veteran campaigners," organizers, or just plain "agitators" whose incomes probably derived wholly or in part from the organizations they helped to lead.

7. See I. B. Tabata, *The Awakening of the People* (London: Spokesman Books, 1974), and idem, *Imperialist Conspiracy* (Lusaka: Prometheus Publishing Company, 1974).

8. For an account favorable to the PAC, see Richard Gibson, *African Liberation Movements: Contemporary Struggles against White Minority Rule* (Oxford: Oxford University Press, 1972). A more recent study is R. W. Johnson, *How Long Will South Africa Survive?* (London: Macmillan, 1977).

9. *African Communist* 43 (1973): 60–61.

10. Ibid., 64 (1976): 30–31.

11. Edward Feit, *African Opposition in South Africa: The Failure of Passive Resistance* (Stanford: Hoover Institution Press, 1967), p. 193. The standard history of the ANC is Peter Walshe, *The Rise of African Nationalism in South*

Africa: The African National Congress, 1912–1952 (Berkeley: University of California Press, 1971).

12. Figures on the extent of African unemployment vary greatly; so does the definition of "unemployment." Estimates range from nine hundred thousand to two million unemployed. The lower figure seems more acceptable but still high. On the other hand, unemployment among Europeans has not assumed major proportions. This disparity between employment figures for whites and blacks—and the disparity in skills and in economic resources available to white and black workers—remain great. Hence outside economic pressure on South Africa, even if it were successful, would hit black workers, the weaker partners in the labor force, with greater severity than Europeans.

Inside South Africa foreign investment has become basically a class issue among blacks, Coloureds, and Indians. Workers, businessmen, and other people who earn their money in the private sector want continued foreign investment. Academics, ministers, welfare workers, and teachers oppose new investments and some even call for divestment. Black trade unionists such as Lucy Mvubelo of the National Union of Clothing Workers calls for more investments because that will mean more jobs for blacks. Chief Gatsha Buthelezi, leader of the Zulus, changed his mind last year about new investments; he now wants economic sanctions to be imposed on South Africa because of the Biko incident, but he is not advocating the withdrawal of companies.

13. Discontent is hard to measure statistically. Much depends on the manner in which public-opinion surveys are conducted, and attitudes are apt to change. Nevertheless, a survey conducted among urban African in Durban in 1975 revealed some strikingly uniform patterns. Africans are discontented, above all, with their economic condition and with racial discrimination. They fear crime even more than they fear the police. Political consciousness is surprisingly poorly developed. Although resentment is widespread, it is not widely directed against the government or the authorities; indeed the authorities and the government rank astonishingly low on the list of "people hated or feared." Only a minority look to organized political action, and an insignificantly small number place their hope in political violence. With regard to wider social attitudes, fear of witches and wizards—once widespread in the countryside—seems to have more or less died out. Urban Africans, on the other hand, express a surprising degree of resentment against ministers of religion, social workers, teachers, doctors, and other elite professionals, who are even more unpopular than chiefs or informers. Some of the more detailed figures from the study follow (since more than one response could be given, percentages exceed 100).

Major Foci of Discontent among Urban Africans in Durban (in percentages)	Educational Level	
	Less than Standard 8	Standard 8 or Above
Discontent with economic conditions	62	62
Discontent about general race discrimination	54	56
Resentment against whites	44	34
Resentment of government or administration	18	21
Discontent about housing, community conditions	10	16
No discontent manifested	6	6

People "Feared and Disliked Most" (in percentages)	Less than Standard 8	Standard 8 or Above
Criminals (gangsters, "tsotsis")	49	46
Police, law enforcers	25	37
Whites	11	10
Ministers of religion, teachers, social workers, doctors	4	15
Other Africans (chiefs, informers, etc.)	9	4
Authorities, government	2	1
Wizards and witches	1	1

Strength of Discontent with Present Conditions (in percentages)	Less than Standard 8	Standard 8 or Above
Emphatic rejection of apartheid, expression of preference for majority rule	71	77
Orientation toward political action, unspecified	17	16
Orientation toward political action, nonconfrontational or nonviolent	13	23
No discontent manifested	6	6
Orientation toward political action, violent	2	1

SOURCE: Lawrence Schlemmer, *Black Attitudes: Reaction and Adaptation* (Durban: University of Natal, Institute for Social Research, 1975), pp. 9, 11, 12.

14. "The Way Forward from Soweto: Political Report Adopted by the Plenary Session of the Central Committee of the South African Communist Party, April 1977," *African Communist* 70 (Third Quarter, 1977): 31–32.

15. See L. H. Gann, *Guerrillas in History* (Stanford: Hoover Institution Press, 1971).

16. According to a statement made by Major General W. Black, head of general operations in the South African Defence Force, South Africa has initially entered the stage of classical insurgency war through internal subversion, sabotage, and terrorism. The enemy will attempt to widen the scope of guerrilla operations with the object of overextending the security forces to such an extent that certain areas could be taken over by the partisans. These regions would then serve as bases to spread the war.

Chapter 5: South Africa in World Politics

1. Conditions as described in "Letter from Robben Island," *Namibia News* 9, no. 9 (September 1976), a strongly anti–South African journal, are vastly better than they would be in a communist prison. Prisoners may study, they receive mail, and they may write letters. They have a prison library at their disposal and they may take correspondence courses. Such conditions would be unthinkable in countries like Angola or Mozambique, but South Africans and Rhodesians have received no credit for their *comparative* humanity. Ndabaningi Sithole, *Obed Mutezo: the Mudzimo Christian Nationalist* (London: Oxford University Press, 1970) has been praised by President Kaunda of Zambia in a preface as an exposi-

tion of "the brutality of the settler security machine." Yet the author explains how political detainees in Rhodesia were able to employ their time usefully by studying for advanced degrees.

As soon as the people had spread themselves, they settled down to study. Advocate Edson Sithole, LL.D., who was serving a twelve-month restriction order, was doing his Master of Laws degree which he eventually passed. Mr. Robert Mugabe, B.A., B.Ed. (S.A.) and B.Sc. (London), was doing his LL.B. also by correspondence. Mr. Edson Zvobogo, B.A. (S.A.), B.A. (Tufts), was also doing LL.B., and most restrictees were doing various courses from Standard Four level to the level of G.C.E. [the British General Certificate of Education].

President Kaunda does not say how many independent African countries would offer similar facilities to political prisoners.

2. Milton Friedman, "South Africa and the Soviet Union," *Newsweek*, 24 May 1976, p. 78. For the wider question of Soviet strategy, see, for instance, Richard Pipes, "Why the Soviet Union Thinks It Could Fight and Win a Nuclear War," *Commentary* 64, no. 1 (July 1977): 21–34.

3. William J. Foltz, "United States Policy toward Southern Africa: Economic and Strategic Constraints," *Politcal Science Quarterly* 92, no. 1 (Spring 1977): 47–64. Foltz claims that there are no substantial economic constraints on American policy toward South Africa. George W. Shepherd, in "The Struggle for a New Southern Africa Policy: The Carter Task," *Journal of Southern African Affairs* 2, no. 1 (January 1977): 99–119, argues for an American alliance with the black independence movements.

Chapter 6: The United States and South Africa

1. George Ball, "Asking for Trouble in South Africa," *Atlantic Monthly* (October 1977): 43–60.

Index

South Africa, for many Americans, is thought to be one of the world's most oppressive countries and a powder keg ready to explode in a racial war. Gann and Duignan show that South Africa is far from the worst government in Africa and that it ranks below all Communist countries in exploiting its people. They consider that with South Africa's defensive potential, defeat in a conventional or guerrilla war or a revolutionary take-over is unlikely. South Africa's power structure is more stable than outsiders believe.

The authors conclude that there will be no South African revolution in our lifetime. Change is more likely to come from within the ruling party than from external liberation movements or a powerless internal opposition. The United States should push for reform and economic development rather than continue the present counter-productive policy of punitive actions and of isolating South Africa.

L.H. Gann   Peter Duignan

Dr. Lewis H. Gann, a senior fellow at the Hoover Institution, Stanford University, is the author of numerous works on the history of Rhodesia, Zambia, European colonialism in Africa, and the development of guerrilla warfare. He holds his B.A. and doctorate from Oxford University and has lived for many years in Africa.

Dr. Peter Duignan, Lillick Curator and head of the Hoover Institution's African program, has published works on the United States and Africa, white settlement in Africa, and colonial rule in Africa. He holds his doctorate from Stanford University, where he formerly taught history.

The two authors have collaborated on many different works, including *Burden of Empire,* a five-volume study of *Colonialism in Africa,* and a trilogy on European colonial elites. Both have traveled extensively in southern Africa and are familiar with its people and their problems.

Richard F. Staar, general editor of this series, is coordinator of international studies at the Hoover Institution. He is author of *Communist Regimes in Eastern Europe,* Third Revised Edition (1977) and editor of the *Yearbook on International Communist Affairs: 1978.*